OH H

The Making of ...

MARIO CONTI

BLACK & WHITE PUBLISHING

First published 2003
by Black & White Publishing Ltd
99 Giles Street, Edinburgh EH6 6BZ

ISBN 1 902927 66 4

A CIP catalogue record for this book
is available from The British Library.

Cover photographs courtesy of Stephen Kearney.
Barga photographs courtesy of Ronnie Convery.
St Peter's Square photographs courtesy of
the *Osservatore Romano*.
All other photographs courtesy of Paul McSherry.

Printed and bound by Creative Print and Design

E chieggioti per quel che tu piu' brami,
se mai calchi la terra di Toscana,
che a' miei propinqui tu ben mi rinfami.

(And I beseech thee, by all thou most desire,
If e'er thou tread the land of Tuscany,
That thou recall my name among my kinsfolk.)

Dante Alighieri, *Purgatorio*, Canto XIII

INTRODUCTION

This is a somewhat rambling account of some of the most memorable days in the first year in the life of an archbishop. Any merit may lie precisely in its rambling nature, since for the rambler it is the small experiences of the countryside with occasional glimpses of the wider landscape which can engage the interest – a particular plant perhaps, or an unusual stone; the way land unfolds to provide a new perspective on what he thought he knew.

For me, there have been predictable experiences and the surprise of the unexpected – a new angle on the role and life of a bishop. All experiences, whether familiar or unexpected, conjure up memories from the past or remind you of things once known but almost forgotten; bits of history, both personal and public.

Inevitably when recalling these things, an element of judgement or discernment enters the picture and I have allowed myself at times to be somewhat self-indulgent in this respect. But I would not like to think that anyone believed these to be anything other than thoughts to be shared in conversation, the sort of thoughts that a rambler may share with his companion as they make their journey together.

One such rambling companion has been Ronnie Convery, my Director of Communications, whose encouragement to respond favourably to the request from the publisher to write this book, and his help in so doing, leave me greatly in his debt.

2001

December

The call comes at about 5.30 p.m. In one sense that is true – I mean the call coming – though, in truth, I had phoned the Apostolic Nunciature (the Papal Ambassador's office) in London, having discovered, on my return from visiting friends near Beauly, that Mgr Jean Marie Speich, the counsellor at the nunciature, has left a message asking me to get in touch.

My name had already been mentioned in connection with Glasgow – somewhat embarrassingly. The first instance had been in the *Scottish Catholic Observer* during the summer of 2000 when there had been speculation as to who might succeed Cardinal Thomas Winning on his eventual retirement. I can vividly recall the heading, 'Aberdeen's loss may be Glasgow's gain', and the reporter had suggested that, perhaps, given the circumstances, it might be appropriate if I were appointed Co-adjutor Archbishop to the Cardinal. I even remember the Cardinal saying to me, as we were walking out of a meeting one day, 'Did you put that report in the *Observer*?' 'No,' I replied, 'I thought you might have!' There was no further comment from him and I did not pursue the matter, though I do confess that, on another occasion, he said to me, 'How would you like to go to Glasgow?'

This carried echoes since he had asked the same question with regard to Aberdeen as we had stood together in 1976 watching the body of my predecessor there, Bishop Michael Foylan, being placed in the hearse. I recall saying something to the effect of 'It would make a nice change!' The fact of the matter was I had been fourteen years in Caithness and, while I was very happy there, did not anticipate staying forever.

So, when I receive the message that I should contact the Nunciature, there is a lurking fear that, perhaps, the call might carry news which would change my life completely. On the other hand, it seems rather soon for such a call to take place. Neither I nor most others anticipate an appointment before Easter, so part of me is saying, 'Don't fear, this is probably about the consultative process or some other matter.'

Content though I am to live in ignorance of the purpose of the call, I cannot delay replying for much longer. And, since everything is now in place for the reception which I am giving this evening in Bishop's House, I decide to call.

Mgr Speich explains that the nuncio, Archbishop Pablo Puente, is away but that he has some important news for me.

'The Holy Father has appointed you Archbishop of Glasgow.'

I don't know whether the word was 'appoint' or 'nominate' or some other expression. All I now remember is that the message struck home.

'Oh Lord!' I reply – less of a prayer and more, I must confess, an expletive. Then there is a longish pause, which probably suggests to the other end of the phone that there is going to be a negative reply.

The conversation commences again with the Counsellor saying, 'But it is a great honour to be Archbishop of Glasgow.' Of that I am sure – it is more than an honour to succeed Cardinal Winning but more of that later.

At this moment I am conscious that I am sixty-seven, going on sixty-eight. I have had, until recent months, the happy expectation of remaining, for however many years the Lord still has in store for me until retirement, as Bishop of Aberdeen. I am looking forward to the silver jubilee of my episcopal ordination, with plans already well afoot, and I had thought that, in the time left to me, I would try to consolidate what has already been achieved. I am looking forward to the development of the Ogilvie Institute, the new adult education centre I have established. And the thought has crossed my mind more than once about where I will go on retirement. Would it be right to stay in Aberdeen or should I return to my native Moray or perhaps find accommodation elsewhere in the diocese where, at some distance from Aberdeen, I might be able to help out pastorally while the Lord continues to give me strength? After all, I have always claimed that the Diocese of Aberdeen is the most beautiful in the country and that is not without some justification as anyone who knows the area will readily concede!

Now all of that is going to change. It is clear in a flash. Will I accept?

When the appointment had merely been a possibility, I had decided that I would say yes if asked. I have always, up to this point, tried whenever possible to say yes to requests. I have also always expected others to accept when, as bishop, I have appointed them to various offices. To have argued incompetence after twenty-five years' experience as a bishop would hardly have borne weight. Unworthiness was not something to be protested since, if others had thought me suited, then any protestations to the contrary might, paradoxically, have argued for false pride rather than humility.

There are, however, two immediate considerations. The first is that the Aberdeen Diocese is well into preparations for my silver jubilee and the second is the realisation that, however willing I might be, the flesh might not be strong enough – in other words, I might need an auxiliary bishop to help me out from the beginning. Glasgow does not have an auxiliary.

So my answer runs along the lines that, while I deeply appreciate that it was an honour to be nominated to Glasgow, I would very much like to have a word with the nuncio before giving my formal consent. It is agreed that I should see him as soon as possible.

I suppose that this little purchase of time eases my mind and will help me to maintain my equilibrium when facing two events which are, under the circumstances, likely to be the last time I will experience them. The first is the reception that lies an hour and a little ahead and the second is the New Year's day dinner which I give annually for the priests of the city and surrounding parishes. That is two days ahead.

Bishop's House at 3 Queen's Cross lends itself to large receptions.

It is a beautifully designed granite villa with its main rooms, on two floors, overlooking what was once a beautifully terraced garden and is now the playground of St Joseph's Catholic Primary School.

The building is now entered, along with the school, from Queen's Road on which it was the first house to be built for an Aberdeen merchant. It takes its address, however, from Queen's Cross, an intersection of five roads over which a brooding statue of Queen Victoria presides. At two of the intersections there are handsome churches serving congregations of the Church of Scotland, opposite to which are, of course, the Catholic primary school and Bishop's House. At another intersection is the former home, now a bank, of George Washington Wilson, the famous Aberdeen photographer.

Once called Westwood Lodge, Bishop's House was built in the middle of the nineteenth century and was later acquired by the nuns of the Society of the Sacred Heart, a Catholic teaching order to which it still belongs. The story goes that the bishop of the time, John MacDonald – the first in the restored bishopric of Aberdeen after the Catholic hierarchy was re-established in Scotland in 1878 – wished the society to establish a school in Aberdeen and not at Nairn, where an enterprising parish priest had sought to have it. Two nuns from the society, dressed in lay clothes, called on the lady of the house and asked to be shown round. They had apparently been given to understand that the house might be for sale. And so, during the course of the tour, they remarked *sotto voce* – but not sufficiently *sotto* not to be overheard – that 'perhaps the other house would be better'. Whether they had considered another house is doubtful but it was a ploy that worked. The lady of the house immediately replied that there wasn't a finer house in Aberdeen, at which she pointed to the doors and asked her two visitors whether they could find any better in the city? Indeed, even today the elegance of design and quality of workmanship is admired, as are so many other architectural details of the interior of the building.

As the nuns left, the lady of the house said, 'Tell your solicitor not to send anyone else' and, sure enough within a short time, the house had been acquired by the Society of the Scared Heart and a community of sisters arrived in what became, for many years, a part-boarding and part-day school for Catholic girls.

It got off to a slow start but the first pupil was a member of the Craigen family, well known then and subsequently in Aberdeen legal circles. She was educated in the room called Bon Accord, a fine room that is divided by sliding doors from a large reception room which was known to many generations of girls as the 'library' – a room, indeed, lined with books from floor to ceiling.

As with so many other convent schools, it expanded rapidly, reflecting, in some ways, the increasing wealth in Victorian society. First of all the sisters built on an additional building of similar proportions to serve as a chapel and classrooms and, then, gradually, they acquired first one, then a second and eventually a third house in Queen's Road. Neighbours must have wondered how many others would be gobbled up. These buildings, now linked together and with the addition of a hall on the other side of the house, form today's St Joseph's and, where once young girls were educated to be ladies, now boisterous youngsters of both sexes fill the corridors and the classrooms.

Each year I still welcome back old girls from the Convent of the Sacred Heart, their interest in what I have done with the house adding significantly to their motivation for attending. However, I also notice how affectionately these former pupils regard the Society. Among them I count my own sister, Stella, who spent some time at Queen's Cross, and my mother, who was educated as a teacher at their training college at St Charles', Kensington. She professed, to her dying day, how much she owed to the Sisters.

When I was a boy at Blairs College, the junior seminary a few miles along the South Deeside Road from Aberdeen, I was allowed to visit my sister, then a boarder at the school. I recall walking with her in the garden under supervision – an evident distraction to the girls playing in the field alongside. This brought back memories for my mother too, who recalled that, even as student teachers, they were chaperoned in the garden at Kensington, adjacent to which there was a boys' school.

When, on my return from studies in Rome in 1959, I was appointed a curate at the cathedral in Aberdeen, I would take my turn, once every three weeks, to celebrate mass for the Sisters at the convent. In those days they wore elegant religious habits, with a finely pleated white cap and diaphanous black veil which billowed slightly as they walked. They were said to have feet but these were none too obvious! The girls were taught to curtsey as they came across a visitor, especially a priest, and it was quite a feat to see how they managed to incorporate this during a headlong dash along the corridor, keeping the rule but not the decorous spirit of it.

At the time, nothing could have been further from my mind than the thought that, one day, I would be living in that convent as Bishop's House. However, by 1996, St Joseph's school had replaced the convent. As the Sisters were no longer members of the staff, they decided to build a new convent in the grounds beyond the playground and this opened up an opportunity for me. With the education authorities not requiring the house at the heart of the school, I was able, under generous provision, to become the tenant of the former convent.

So it is that, on this fateful day, following a practice I had established at my previous residence, King's Gate, I welcome to Bon Accord and the former library some seventy guests, representing various Catholic groups and organisations in the city and friends from within and from outside the Catholic community, including the new Solicitor General for Scotland, Elish Angiolini. (On a previous occasion I had welcomed Jim Leighton OBE, for many years Aberdeen's trusty goalkeeper. It gave me considerable pleasure to see him taking up the collection in one of our parishes for, as someone remarked, 'It was in safe hands!')

There is wine in plenty as well as a wide variety of savouries, for the production of which my former housekeeper, Jean Johnstone, returned from her retirement home in Fochabers. Jean had been my housekeeper at King's Gate after returning from voluntary service with the Catholic Church in Canada. Before that, as a girl, she had been a pupil at Queen's Cross and she rejoiced at the turn of events!

It would have been a most appropriate occasion at which to announce the news that I have just received. However, that was not permitted and it may, indeed, have put a damper on the evening since what from one angle might have given pleasure, from another might well have caused some sadness – the sadness which would undoubtedly come when I had to take leave of those whose bishop I had been for twenty-five years.

Hogmanay: Monday, 31 December

Today I have a chance to try to come to terms with the import of yesterday's message. As I gather up the many gifts and, particularly, the bottles of wine which, in good Scots fashion, my visitors had brought, I can not help but think and wonder where and on what occasion I would be opening them.

For years I have taken in the New Year with my former neighbours at King's Gate and, even after having moved to Queen's Cross I had maintained my connection with them. They are a splendid company of people – both native Aberdonians and incomers to the city – and the tradition had been established years before that my next-door neighbour, Mrs Betty Petrie, a widow, would invite us all in for a Hogmanay drink and savouries, the event later being extended to include a full buffet supper to which all neighbours contributed.

I arrive as usual with my bottle and greet everyone – the only person there realising the heightened significance of this particular New Year for one of the company. The custom has also grown of us visiting one or two of the neighbours' houses in order to first foot them. And so it is from the home of James and Muriel Cameron – the man who had once welcomed me as Deacon Convenor to the prestigious annual Guilds Dinner at Trinity Hall – that I return home.

2002

January

Tuesday, 1 January

I celebrate mass this morning in St Mary's Cathedral, the elegant granite mother church of the Diocese of Aberdeen, with its tapering spire and fine façade, just a couple of hundred yards from Union Street.

As usual a smallish but devout congregation has gathered to dedicate the first day of the year to the Lord and to pray for peace. I can give no hint of my appointment to the administrator of the cathedral, Fr Andrew Mann, also from my part of the world, nor to the dozen or so members of the clergy who arrive at my house subsequently for what has also become an annual event – namely, the dinner for the priests of the city and surrounding parishes.

We sit round the large table that had once stood in the professors' dining room at Blairs. For this reason I called the room, which could be used both for conferences and for dining, the Blairs Room. Over the mantelpiece is a painting on loan from the Blairs Museum – a very fine copy painted on slate from a French atelier of a painting by Raphael of the Christ child and St John the Baptist. I have recently had it cleaned and it looks spectacular. On another wall is a large photograph of Blairs College's baronial entrance tower and its elegant chapel spire silhouetted against a winter sky. This is matched by a replica of the Bull of Foundation of the University of Aberdeen, established in 1495 by a medieval predecessor, Bishop William Elphinstone and Pope Alexander VI. Given the notoriety of this Borgia pope, I used to joke that, in all probability, Aberdeen was the only place in the world where Alexander VI is portrayed in stained glass!

To return to the table, I recall, many years ago as a bishop, being a guest of my colleague in Edinburgh, Archbishop Keith Patrick O'Brien, who was then Rector of Blairs. Opposite me at table was a Carmelite nun who, in a rare gesture of indulgence, had been allowed out of her enclosure in order to visit a nephew who was in Peterhead Prison. Freed from the austerities of the Carmelite regime, she appeared to be enjoying not only the company but the food and the unaccustomed wine.

Her pink cheeks indicating that perhaps she had had enough, the rector suggested to her that there would be no discourtesy in her leaving and going to her room since, he said, 'I do not know what the rule says.'

'Oh,' she said, 'Our Mother Teresa did not foresee such an occasion and so did not make a rule about it!'

Many a tale that table could tell were it able to speak and many a judgement secretly overheard it could report on students past and present, including possibly those of the present hierarchy, half of whom were boys at Blairs. As one such former student, I recall the day when the then-rector, Gordon Gray, was announced as the new Archbishop of St Andrews and Edinburgh. The students were high with excitement and, at lunch in the refectory below the professors' dining room, they launched into song after song, cleverly alluding in one way or another to the appointment. Songs were sung such as 'The Old Grey Mare he Ain't What he Used to Be' and 'There's a Toorie on his Bonnet, a Red Toorie on It'. Eventually the Master of Discipline appeared, himself subsequently to be rector both of the Royal Scots College in Spain and the Pontifical Scots College in Rome. He announced a decree that there was to be no more singing in the refectory, with the sole exception of 'Happy Birthday' – a consoling concession.

Hardly had he left when the student body sang 'Happy Birthday' to the new archbishop, to a dozen students chosen at random, to the cat, the dog and the budgerigar! The students may have lost the battle but they appeared to have won the war!

It is round that same table that we gather today for a meal, generously prepared as ever by Jean, and for what I alone know is to be my last dinner with the Aberdeen clergy at New Year. Perhaps my successor will feel obliged to continue the tradition.

JANUARY

Friday, 4 January

Today I go to Peterhead Prison to visit the inmates. The chaplain – one much loved by those who feel he has sympathy for them and never speaks down to them – is Fr Raymond Coyle, parish priest at Ellon, and he introduces me to the governor and staff over a buffet lunch. They are ready to tell me and I am ready to hear that the work on rehabilitation of sex offenders, which has been developed at Peterhead, is regarded, not only in this country but also abroad, as exemplary. The concern they express is that, for financial reasons, Peterhead will be closed. I readily agree that, once a programme has taken root in a place after much effort and experience, it cannot easily be transplanted elsewhere and I promise to support their case. I will invite our Parliamentary Officer, John Deighan, to represent our concerns to parliamentarians.

I celebrate mass for the Catholic prisoners and others who join them and we chat afterwards over tea and biscuits in an adjoining room.

Wednesday, 9 January

Because I am due in London tomorrow to attend a meeting of the Catholic Bishops Joint Bioethics Committee at the Linacre Centre, I am able – after excuses and cancelling only one appointment – to come to London today to meet the apostolic nuncio. I am met at Heathrow by the nuncio's chaplain, Mgr Peter Grant, a priest from the north of England who travels with him and helps steer him through the unknown byways of British life.

The nuncio is the pope's ambassador to the Court of St James. The papal ambassador was traditionally given this title although, at one time, he was called pro-nuncio in Britain – a title given to those nuncios who did not, as in Catholic countries following the Congress of Vienna, automatically act as deans of the diplomatic corps. That Congress, which in some ways reconstructed Europe after Napoleon, not inappropriately recognised the *primus inter pares* (first among equals status) of the papal nuncio, since the great Cardinal Ercole Consalvi, nuncio to Paris in Napoleon's time, alone appeared to stand in front of the Emperor and question him. Consalvi, a cleric but not a bishop, became secretary of state to Pope Pius VII and had his office in the magnificent Consulta Palace adjacent to the Quirinal in Rome – a more beautiful complex of palaces hardly being imaginable.

Now every nuncio is an archbishop and the one I am visiting, Pablo Puente, is a Spaniard by birth who, after a distinguished diplomatic career which saw him serve in the Vatican's embassies to Paraguay, Santo Domingo, Kenya, Tanzania, Lebanon, Yugoslavia, Indonesia, Senegal, Mali, Cape Verde, Mauritania, Guinea-Bissau, Kuwait and the Arabian peninsula, was appointed to London in 1997.

The last time I was in the nunciature was during the time of his predecessor, the Swiss Archbishop Bruno Heim. That visit and that nuncio come strongly back to mind as I am ushered into the elegant house and asked to wait in a conservatory area which I recall was once filled with potted plants. It was precisely here – after a meal during which I had been embarrassed by a number of questions, the import of which I did not understand, and where I had been seated first on one side then, when it was clear that I was against the light, on the other – that I was asked the question: 'Why do you think you are here?'

I started to reply, 'I suppose to be . . . ', the word 'pumped' came to mind but I thought it undiplomatic language and it was precisely in that moment of hesitation that I heard him say, 'You are the new Bishop of Aberdeen!' That was twenty-five years ago almost to the day.

I rehearse in my mind the questions I want to ask before giving what, by now, seems an almost inevitable assent to my appointment as Archbishop of Glasgow. This time it is Archbishop Puente who arrives and takes me into a neighbouring reception room where he sits me down.

The first question is whether, given my age and the enormity of the task that lay ahead, I would be likely to be given the assistance of an auxiliary bishop. I suppose the real question underlying this is one that might have been couched in such language as, 'Do you really think I'm able to do this task?' The nuncio senses this and, after saying that he does not think there would be any difficulty about an affirmative answer to my request, says he is sure that I I will have the backing of my colleagues and can expect a welcome from the priests of the Archdiocese of Glasgow.

Having been so comforted, I then ask the second question, which matters more to me perhaps than to him or, indeed, anyone else other than my diocesans in Aberdeen – namely, if I were appointed to Glasgow, could I still return to Aberdeen for the celebration of my silver jubilee which has been long planned and is due to take place on the anniversary of my ordination as a bishop on 3 May? The nuncio says that it is unlikely that an appointment will be made to Aberdeen by that time – something that I hardly need assurance of – and he sees no difficulty about my returning for the celebration. I know that this will be one of the first questions I will be asked in Aberdeen and I am happy that I can now respond to it positively with the assurance of the nuncio's support.

He looks at the calendar and suggests that the publication of the news could be made early next week – either on the Monday or Tuesday. I opt for the Tuesday, thinking that it will give me a better opportunity to travel to Glasgow since I have an appointment for mass on Sunday. I have only one remaining appointment which I need to find a reason to change and so maintain the secrecy which the nuncio considers important – indeed, so important that, on inquiring as to whether I could mention it to my sister whom I would be seeing this evening, he replies in the negative.

'No one must be told.'

He informs me that he himself will speak to the Chancellor of the Archdiocese, Mgr Peter Smith, and the Administrator, Mgr John Gilmartin. No doubt they will then be in touch with me in order to make arrangements for the announcement which is to be at precisely 11 o'clock next Tuesday – midday Roman time. He also encourages me to think of an early date for my formal installation. After a light lunch, he bids goodbye to me for the time being. I am taken once more by the nuncio's car, again accompanied by Mgr Peter Grant, to Euston to catch a train for Solihull.

I have time on this journey to mull over all that has happened and to reflect again on the extraordinary character of the apostolic nuncio. I don't mean his personal character as much as the character of his office. He is the pope's man in Britain and, as such, relates to the bishops of England, Wales, Scotland and Northern Ireland – a conduit of information rather like Jacob's ladder on which the angels ascend and descend! One of his most important ecclesiastical tasks is to provide, after very discreet and exhaustive inquiry, the names of those candidates who are considered suitable for appointment to vacant dioceses. The practice is to send a 'terna', a list of three names in order of preference, to the Con-gregation for Bishops in Rome.

He is also the natural contact person between the Vatican and the UK and, until 1982, when he was given full ambassadorial rank, was called the apostolic delegate. The Holy See exchanges ambassadors with more than 170 countries, a testimony to the Vatican's supra-national identity and moral authority. Despite the smallness of its territorial sovereignty which amounts to just a few acres, it is filled nonetheless with some of the greatest monuments to human artistry and invention. Its library and archives contain innumerable documents plotting the history of mankind and, given the universal character of the Catholic Church, many opine that it has probably the best-informed diplomatic corps of any state.

I arrive at Solihill and am met by my brother-in-law, Noel Minihan. He and my sister, Stella, have a flat nearby and I go there to spend the evening with them, dissembling my purpose in taking a flight from London and not Birmingham on the basis of convenience. I could use my return ticket direct from the capital.

Naturally I would like to have given the news to my sister this evening. I would also have liked to tell the friends I am due to meet back in London tomorrow at the Linacre Centre – including bishops I hope will eventually attend my installation.

All this secrecy will soon be at an end. It is all cloak-and-dagger stuff though, on reflection, I think perhaps this is not the most apt expression. Let's just say it is 'Pontifical secret stuff'!

The whole process by which a bishop is nominated, has his credentials examined, has letters of commendation sought and his appointment communicated is covered by the phrase 'Pontifical secrecy'. Dire penalties are threatened for anyone who breaks this bond. It may seem to some unduly restraining but it does have the advantage of avoiding any lobbying for candidates, joining forces to press their case and producing leaks, all to the embarrassment of those who are appointed and those who are not.

The clergy have a way of getting round this to some extent by not communicating the fact that they have been asked by the nuncio for their opinion about this or that person. Subterfuges are employed such as I know were used in my own case before being appointed as Bishop of Aberdeen, with members of the clergy asking one another 'How do you spell "Conti"?'! The candidate is, of course, the one least likely to hear such questions and can, therefore, remain an innocent until the moment of revelation.

I am not permitted to pass on this revelation to anyone. On the other hand, Mgr Peter Smith, Chancellor of the Archdiocese of Glasgow, has been informed and advised to make all the necessary arrangements for the announcement in a couple of days' time.

Thursday, 10 January

I'm off again – yesterday's train but in the opposite direction. From Euston I take the underground to St John's Wood and the Linacre Centre. It has rooms in what was formerly the Convent of Mercy, whose sisters once staffed the adjoining hospital of St John and St Elizabeth. This still exists as a private hospital but is managed now by the Sovereign Military and Hospitaller Order of St John of Jerusalem, Rhodes and Malta – better known as the Knights of Malta.

Like the Holy See, this great international order is a sovereign legal entity, recognised mainly by Catholic nations with which it exchanges ambassadors. It originated 900 years ago in the work of Blessed Gerard and his companions, who maintained a hospital for pilgrims in Jerusalem. To this day, its flag of a white cross on a red background – the reverse of the red cross – identifies it with the Italian seaport of Amalfi, once an important seafaring community in the south-west of Italy to which Blessed Gerard belonged.

The Linacre Centre is a much more recent establishment, having been set up in 1977. Through its research, teaching, publications and consultancy work, it gives valuable service to the Catholic community in Great Britain, Ireland and further afield, as well as to the wider community, especially through its contribution to public policy debates. Over the years it has acquired an international reputation for reliable scholarship in the field of healthcare ethics.

It is appropriate, therefore, that the Catholic Bishops Joint Bioethics Committee – a committee set up by the Catholic Bishops of England, Wales, Scotland and Ireland – should meet there. Its purpose is similar – namely, to address the medical moral issues of the day and to provide advice to bishops and the Catholic faithful, as well as contributing to public policy debates. It is an interdisciplinary committee, comprised of only two bishops from each of the conferences represented but also of moral theologians and medical, legal and other professionals with a concern in the field of medical ethics.

My predecessor, Cardinal Winning, was for many years its chairman, though I do recall on one occasion taking the chair in his absence and being very impressed at the unanimity of view reached from the various specialist angles of those present. The question, on that occasion, was whether it was ever moral to withdraw such primary care as nourishment and hydration from a patient in a so-called persistent vegetative state. We concluded unanimously that it was not. To withdraw such treatment was to bring about the death of the patient deliberately. There are, of course, many other circumstances, such as the removal of artificial ventilation and the discontinuation of non-rehabilitative treatment and drugs, when such actions are justified. There comes a time when we must let nature take its course. It is often then that the palliative care provided by hospices takes over.

Round the table today are bishops, colleagues and friends whom I cannot advise of my impending appointment but whom I hope will join me for my installation as archbishop. I sense that the education I receive in this group and the support I depend upon will serve me well in the future.

I am not above taking advantage of their expertise sometimes. I recall, on one occasion, asking the former president of the Royal College of Geriatricians, Prof. Peter Millard, why it was that some people on retirement seem to 'pop off' quickly while others, not retiring, went on for ages. He said it was all to do with traction. This aroused the interest of those round about and simultaneously formed in my mind the image of some poor creature being put on the rack – you sometimes see it in orthopaedic wards: arms being held up by weights and legs apparently stretched by similar means. However, on further inquiry, he explained that what he meant was 'being forever drawn to the next task'. I will, no doubt, think of this during the course of the coming year!

Friday, 11 January

I came back last night from London and I drive up today to celebrate a mass of thanksgiving at Buckie. The parish priest, Mgr Eddie Traynor, my vicar general, has recovered marvellously from what seemed a terminal illness. The church at Buckie, with its twin spires, was clearly inspired by the plan of Elgin Catheral nearby, once the seat of the Bishops of Moray. When St Peter's, Buckie, was built a few years before St Mary's Cathedral in Aberdeen, it was half expected that it might eventually, on the restoration of the Catholic hierarchy, be the cathedral of the diocese. It was in this area, as well as in the Western Isles of Scotland and one or two remote Highland glens, that the remnant of the Catholic Church survived during its darkest days in post-Reformation Scotland.

After the mass, we all repair to the Fisherman's Hall for a social. I stay overnight at Buckie.

Saturday, 12 January

I set off for Aberdeen, calling in, en route, to see Mgr John Copland, the former vicar general. After a long struggle with cancer, he is now in the Keith Cottage Hospital. I sense it will be my last meeting with him. He is being well cared for and I leave comforted on that score, though saddened to see his deterioration in health.

Insofar as I am now on my journey to Glasgow, it seems appropriate that I should be starting it from the Braes of Enzie, the area from which so many post-Reformation priests came, some of whom became vicars apostolic (leaders of the Church during the period prior to the restoration of the Hierarchy in 1878). Among them was Andrew Scott, whose chapel on the banks of the Clyde is to become my new cathedral church.

My appointment is going to be earlier than expected and not only the press but members of the archdiocese will be caught on the hop. The administrator, for example, is absent for a post-Christmas break and, in the event, it will be another member of the College of Consultors, Fr Neil Donnachie, Rector of Scotus College, who will introduce me.

I have, of course, been in contact with Mgr Peter Smith and, when I arrive, it has been decided that I will stay overnight in St Gabriel's Parish House where he has his own accommodation. The parish priest, Fr Michael Woodford, is going to be absent and so there is little chance of my being observed and raising any alarm!

Monday, 14 January

I arrived back in Aberdeen yesterday and have one more function to fulfil here before I leave for Glasgow later in the afternoon. I am to attend the funeral of Cllr Bob Middleton, a long-standing Labour councillor and leader who served both on Aberdeen District Council and Grampian Regional Council, being sometime convenor of Grampian. I always got on well with Bob and he and his wife, Audrey, have been guests at my home at Queen's Cross. In fact, Audrey had, for many years, been Secretary at St Joseph's School, of which, in a sense, Queen's Cross was the core.

Bob was, I imagine, 'Old Labour' by temperament and conviction. A doughty fighter, he was also a very fair man and I recall my meeting with him when negotiations were taking place between the Council and the Society of the Sacred Heart for a renewed lease on the premises. It was Bob who had then encouraged me to think of occupying the former convent.

There is a great turnout at Aberdeen Conference Centre for his funeral and everybody in public positions in the city and region is there. I recognise many and greet friends, thinking that this is perhaps a goodbye, though they do not realise it.

Bob had not been a religious man in the conventional sense but he respected the cloth, as they say, and his family had reserved a place for me in the front row. Instead of a hymn, we sing 'A Man's a Man for A' That' and never did it seem more appropriate than on this occasion.

Being in the front row, I am able to make an early exit and, therefore, be at the top of the queue for signing the book of condolence. I am conscious that I am signing my name for the last time as '+Mario Conti, Bishop of Aberdeen'.

I take the train this afternoon, the 15. 38 from Aberdeen Station, and arrive in Glasgow at 18.15 where Mgr Peter Smith is waiting for me. His presence is a comforting sight. I am already aware of his loyalty to my predecessor and of his great efficiency, and I know that everything will be in order. And so it is – except, perhaps, for the room that I have in the presbytry which is in a state of half occupancy. I share it with piles of furniture which are still looking for their proper place, so it is like coming into the archdiocese through a glory hole!

Once before I entered through a glory hole. I was visiting a museum in northern Italy when I realised that everybody had disappeared and that the gates and doors were locked. It was then

27

that the storyline from a comic helped me out. I recalled seeing a balloon above the head of Mickey Mouse, when he was in one of his regular predicaments, with the word '*Aiuto!*' which means 'Help!'. Well, I started shouting '*Aiuto!*' and banging on the door until someone still in the building heard me and rescued me via a broom cupboard.

Tuesday, 15 January

Early this morning I have the first experience of a form of terror. I think this may have been as much related to the anticipated attention of the press and numerous interviews I will be expected to give following the announcement, as to the enormity of what I am undertaking. But I am calm by the time our concelebrated mass in the parish church next door is over, not least because of the warmth shown to me by parishioners who do not know – though some may have suspected – what is to transpire that very day. However, as yet, no news has been given to the media of the press conference that we are ready to call for 11 o'clock, the time of the midday announcement in Rome.

By the time Mgr Peter and I arrive at the back door of the Curial Offices in Clyde Street, this information has been made public.

'I think George suspects something,' says Mgr Peter as we arrive. George is the janitor and general handyman who is noted for the general alertness – essential to someone in that position – he shows to all that is going on. As sure as fate, we meet him as we creep through the foyer. He gives us a knowing look.

At the information desk this morning is a temp – someone filling in for Eileen, the receptionist who was absent. Never was a temp to experience a more unexpectedly interesting day! Trying to be helpful later on, she responds to an inquiry as to who the new archbishop is to be by saying she has no idea but that she has overheard a conversation and thought it might be . . . She names one of my fellow bishops, whose name is, therefore, mentioned on the radio a short while prior to the actual announcement – much, I suspect, to the embarrassment of the individual himself who, according to reports, is disturbed in his office by someone rushing in to congratulate him!

We get upstairs, otherwise unseen. The element of surprise is, therefore, still a possibility.

Sitting in the archbishop's office, which last I had been in after the funeral of my predecessor, Cardinal Winning, is a somewhat strange experience. Here am I, the new archbishop, and yet no one knows. I am sitting in an office that is now mine but apparently as a visitor. All is quiet but it is the lull before the storm. As the moments tick by to 11 o'clock, I reflect on all that I might be asked and how I might respond. I assume questions would relate to how I feel succeeding Cardinal Tom. Would I adopt his style or would there be a change both of style and emphasis? If there is to be a change, then what will it be?

I haven't really anticipated questions such as, 'How would you describe yourself?' Perhaps that is just as well because it leads to some spontaneity when eventually they come. 'Charming,' I say to one interviewer, perhaps rather cheekily, when she poses that question but, by that time, the worst is over and I am beginning to relax.

However, that is somewhat ahead. It suddenly occurrs to me that I feel a bit like Mary, Queen of Scots, awaiting the executioner – perhaps a somewhat strange sort of comparison but, when Mgr Peter, eventually entering, says, 'I feel like the executioner taking Mary, Queen of Scots, on her final journey', I begin to think that, perhaps, there is something in the comparison after all! It is strange, though, that still, within the Scottish Catholic mindset, the memory of Mary as a martyr for the faith should readily come to mind.

'Just what I was thinking, Peter,' I reply and the amusement helps to restore some normality to what is a most unusual experience.

Just then the late Cardinal's Director of Communications and Researcher, Ronnie Convery, comes into the room, along with Peter Kearney, our recently appointed Director of the Catholic Media Office for whom this is his first big test – as it is mine! They can now be told and the genuine warmth of their expression prompts me to embrace both of them. There are times when such human contact, less commonplace here than on the Continent, seems absolutely right and provides that reassurance that we not infrequently need.

Down we go together to the Eyre Hall on the first floor. We go in and all eyes dart from one to the other as this small procession makes its way to the dais at the end. Perhaps not all members of the press corps are sufficiently familiar with the Church personnel to be able to deduce immediately who is the new archbishop, but the more informed eyes of the office staff do not leave their owners in any doubt. A process of elimination in such circumstances is fairly easy!

We sit down. A welcome is given to staff and press and the formal announcement is made. I think there is some applause but what I am conscious of is that all eyes are now on me and follow me as I make my way to the reading desk. I have prepared a short statement – so short that it fits on to a postcard.

I have to ad-lib a bit, saying what is probably evident to all there, that Cardinal Tom 'is a hard act to follow'. This sound bite is everywhere to be found, thereafter – as is my tongue-in-cheek response later to an interviewer who asks about my readiness to tackle sectarianism in the west of Scotland: 'I come as an innocent from the north-east.'

I am photographed from this angle and that, against this background and that, in front of the portrait of my predecessor hanging, along with other distinguished holders of the office of Archbishop of Glasgow, from the time of Archbishop Eyre after whom the hall was named. I am interviewed by this person and that one and, at the end of it all, am exhausted but greatly relieved. I am going to be given a chance to prove myself. For the moment the press seems to be kind – very kind indeed.

It is clear to me, as it is to others, that the sort of attention my appointment receives would not have been of the same magnitude had it not been for the public persona of Cardinal Tom. He may often have felt that he had been mauled by the press but he remained typically up-front with them, giving them the sort of sound bites they wanted and, in the end, they loved him. The evidence was seen at the time of his funeral. The fear that he had expressed some time before his death that 'I worry that my family might be hurt by what they write about me when I'm dead' proved to be quite groundless. Anyone with any experience of the media recognises that it can be generous, that it can put someone on a pedestal for a while, only to knock him off at the first opportunity and, of course, the higher the pedestal, the greater the fall. I am determined not to be put on a pedestal. It is true that Humpty-Dumpty can sometimes be put together again but it is little consolation to one who is living to know that this might not happen until after death!

From the beginning I have realised that, after the first hurdle of the press conference has been overcome, the next big one is the actual induction. It used to be called 'enthronement' but now the word used might be 'installation' or 'inauguration' – the former rather suggesting the leading of a willing or less willing animal to its stall.

The Speaker of the House of Commons is expected to show reluctance at his 'installation' and, I suppose, some measure of that is not unbecoming as a sign of due humility at being placed in a somewhat elevated position – even if elevated by only a step. To the frequent expressions of congratulation on my 'elevation', I have tended to respond that 'I am now on the fourth floor and have an elevator!' That, of course, refers to my office next to the cathedral with its lovely views south across the Clyde. With windows all round it reminds me of a ship's bridge – perhaps not an inappropriate description given the typical role of a bishop to 'oversee'. Hence the word 'episcope', from which we get the word 'bishop'.

The cathedral, on the other hand, draws its name from the chair or 'cathedra', a symbol of a bishop's office as teacher and presider, and it is to that chair that my focus is now turned, although I decide not to see it until the day comes for me to take possession of it.

It had been left empty at the Cardinal's funeral, though it could have been used by the presiding bishop, who, on that occasion, was the Archbishop of Westminster – a Cardinal doing his duty for a fellow member of the Sacred College. No one has sat on it since the Cardinal's last celebration in the cathedral, unless naughty altar boys, when backs were turned, had tried it out for size! It was once the custom in medieval times for a boy bishop to be given all the trappings of episcopal office for a day, including that of sitting on the bishop's throne and leading a procession through the town with mitre and crozier. In these less ecclesiastically minded days, I suppose our gala queen and her princess attendants are doing something similar. I'm sure the Queen doesn't bat an eyelid at such shows any more than the bishops of old, who must have taken part in some way as conspirators in this enjoyment.

My thought now, as the day ends, is to get back to Aberdeen – to creep home, almost surreptitiously, hoping that nobody connects the cleric in the coach with the news which is even now being broadcast of the appointment of a successor to Cardinal Winning.

Wednesday, 16 January

Today I have to face the music. I have to apologise to my secretaries for not giving them a hint, though I suspect my PA, Irene Melling, had an inkling. Tom Cooney, Aberdeen's Diocesan Communications Officer, arrives to report on how the media has handled things – we agree generously. At twelve noon I am interviewed for Radio Scotland and, in the afternoon at 2.30 p.m., I have a meeting of the managers of the Blairs Museum, a project dear to me since it prevented the dispersal of the paintings, vestments and other treasures of the Church which had accumulated over the years at the former junior seminary.

The most famous item in that collection is the so-called 'memorial' portrait of Mary, Queen of Scots. It shows Mary as she was dressed on the day of her execution. She holds a gold crucifix in her hand and, depicted around her, are scenes from Fotheringay

Castle where she was beheaded as the enemy of Elizabeth I and of her religion.

It was painted by a Flemish artist apparently from a miniature given by the ill-fated queen to Elizabeth Curle, a lady-in-waiting, whose relative was a Jesuit member of staff at the Scots College at Douai for which the painting was intended. When so much else was lost at the time of the French Revolution, whether at the Scots College in Paris or that at Douai, this painting marvellously escaped by being rolled up and pushed up a chimney. Thank goodness no one lit a fire!

We have a report on the condition of the painting that is in Edinburgh to be cleaned. Apparently, many fine details are emerging from the thick varnish and grime of the years (and perhaps the soot of the chimney!).

Thursday, 17 January

There is a meeting this morning of the so-called Regional Ecumenical Team, comprising church leaders and representatives of the churches in Aberdeen. Over the years, we have worked so closely together that inevitably their coming this morning and their words of encouragement mean a very great deal to me.

In the afternoon, I travel south again – this time to Edinburgh from where I leave for a formal visitation of the Pontifical Scots College in Rome tomorrow. My colleague is the Archbishop of St Andrews and Edinburgh, the Most Rev. Keith Patrick O'Brien, and he has very kindly gathered a group of Edinburgh priests together and, with them, surprised me with a splendid dinner earlier this evening on the eve of our departure. I expected some supper but not the magnificent spread prepared by Theresa, his housekeeper, nor the excellent company that the archbishop has assembled.

It is a most gracious welcome to me in my new position and immediately gives the lie to any predicted rivalry on the part of two archbishops whose cities are notoriously said to eye one another with suspicion and jealousy.

Friday, 18 January

Archbishop Keith and I leave for Rome where we are met by a member of staff at the Scots College. I dare say that, as an alumnus of that historic establishment, there is an extra special element to the welcome given to me and I suppose it is to be expected that I would be greeted in the refectory with a round of applause!

The next week is to be spent here in Rome. Our visit is to ensure that the college is being faithful to its mission of training young men for the priesthood and this involves interviewing, individually, the members of the staff, the student body and the group of ten or so post-graduate priests also sharing the building – the majority of whom come from Africa and Asia.

I soon make the acquaintance of the four students for the priest-hood studying in Rome for the Archdiocese of Glasgow. They are joined by another, Frank Wilson, studying at the Pontifical Beda College – a college adapted to men of more mature years, many of them converted clergymen. Frank, however, was a medical doctor and had exercised his profession for many years as a GP in Glasgow.

Monday, 21 January

Today is an outstanding one as far as I am concerned. It starts with a visit, in the company of Archbishop Keith, to Sant'Agnese Fuori le Mura – literally, the Church of St Agnes 'outside the walls'. This is an ancient basilica on the Via Nomentana, built over the grave of a famous young Roman martyr, Agnes. She was little more than a girl when she was put to death for stubbornly holding to her faith and apparently attempting to resist the sexual advances of either a Roman official or his son – it is not very clear.

However, a lovely tradition has developed around it on this day – the Feast of St Agnes, whereby two lambs are blessed. Though her name is from the Greek meaning 'holiness', the Latin for a lamb, 'agnus', appropriately associates the sacrificial nature of their death with her. Since Agnes was both a virgin and a martyr, one of the lambs in this ceremony stands for her virginity and the other her martyrdom. One lamb, therefore, sits with the letters

'SAV' – Saint Agnes Virgin – in a basket of white flowers and with a white wreath on its head, while the other, similarly adorned in red flowers and accompanied by the letters 'SAM' – Saint Agnes Martyr – sits in another. (I must confess, however, that, when Archbishop Keith O'Brien and I first noticed the letters 'SAM', we thought that this must be the lamb's pet name. 'SAV', of course, made no sense until we eventually discovered its real significance.)

These two lambs are all ready to be taken, in procession, down the long corridor leading to the church, which is in part below street level and from which it is still possible to go even lower to connect with part of an old Roman catacomb where the early Christians buried their dead.

After the mass, which, unfortunately, we cannot wait for, the lambs are presented to the pope, who then sees that they are taken to the papal farm at Castel Gandolfo. When they are sheared in early summer, their wool will be given to the Benedictine nuns at Trastevere to be woven into the pallia or badges of office of metropolitan archbishops. These are then placed on the tomb of St Peter, before being taken to the Holy Father who invests the new archbishops present in Rome for the great Feast of Saints Peter and Paul. Those unable to be in attendance have their pallia sent to them. My predecessor received his by courier relay – the last bearer leaving the box on the window ledge as Archbishop Winning (as he was then) was not at home!

It is to St Peter's that Archbishop Keith and I now go. For me this means a visit to Cardinal Giovanni Battista Re, the Prefect of the Congregation for Bishops in the Vatican. His office is at the top of the Via della Conciliazione, immediately in front of Bernini's colonnade and the Piazza San Pietro.

I enter such august premises with some trepidation but, when the door is thrown open and this extrovert prelate comes in, it is all friendship and benevolence. Putting his arm around me, he says, 'Ma Lei ha un solo difetto' – 'You have only one defect'. And then he pauses to see my reaction. Of course, in the few seconds between his remark and what follows I wonder what he might have in mind. Surely not my theology? After all, I was Roman-trained. Perhaps my age? I am rather near the end of eligibility in that respect. Of what crime am I unwittingly guilty? Then comes his response: *'Suo nome!'* – 'Your name!'. I try to explain that having an Italian name in Scotland is not a particularly rare thing, there being families of Italian descent in almost every self-respecting town and village in the country. However, he makes it clear he was joking.

Then we get down to business, which involves my making a solemn act of faith and taking the oath of allegiance that is required of every priest in the Church who assumes a new pastoral responsibility. I am gently hauled along to the little chapel – 'Not grand like your cathedral' – where, kneeling on a plush prie-dieu with Cardinal Re and his secretary looming over me, I am handed the Latin text of the Creed and the Oath of Fidelity. In such awesome circumstances, it is good that I have had seven years of Latin lectures and exams, as well as the memory of Latin masses wherein the Creed had been recited regularly, to ensure that I get through it all without stumbling. Pity, I think, for those who, much younger than I, would come to such a moment with less preparation!

All I have to do now is to sign a document, which I think I do legibly. More bonhomie and I am back in the square among the pilgrims who are none the wiser that, here among them, is a fledgling archbishop who has just made that momentous act of faith on which the Church is built.

Thursday, 24 January
I get back from Rome via Edinburgh today and I'm glad to be home since I have the beginnings of a cold. So often one gets these colds when travelling by air. I'm glad to be home for another reason too. This weekend we have a distinguished visitor in Aberdeen in the person of Jean Vanier.

Saturday, 26 January
'Faith,' says St James, 'is dead without good deeds' (Jas. 2: 26). Jean

Vanier is a man whose faith has produced the marvellous work of L'Arche, a movement for the care of those we once called the handicapped, those the Italians still call *'gli handicappati'* in direct transliteration. Leaders, helpers and those who are partially disadvantaged live together, in a sort of large, extended family, and there are several such houses in Inverness.

I welcome Jean to the vigil mass at the cathedral where he addresses the congregation with exemplary brevity and powerful effect. One thinks of charisma in such cases – a word that enfolds the Greek word for 'grace'.

Sunday, 27 January – Monday, 28 January

It is an actual grace for all of us who hear Jean Vanier, either at St Mary's last night or today at the ecumenical service in the packed Music Hall, just a stone's throw from the cathedral.

Everywhere I go these days I am greeted with warm congratulations. How supportive such gestures and words can be but what expectations they tend to raise! I rush from the Music Hall to the airport to catch a plane for Shetland and the festival of Up-Helly-Aa.

If I had known last year on my previous visit to the most northerly parish in Scotland, St Margaret's, Lerwick, that, in January, I would be appointed Archbishop of Glasgow, I would certainly not have taken on this particular engagement which means dedicating three full days to it out of the short time left to me in Aberdeen. What no one could anticipate, however, is having a killer of a cold and so my days in Shetland are spent with a running nose more suited to Rudolph the Red Nosed Reindeer than the newly appointed Archbishop of Glasgow! The weather is, of course, seasonably cold with a cutting wind which takes every opportunity to penetrate layers of clothing as one stands to watch outdoor processions in the most exposed places.

I am met in Lerwick by the parish priest, Fr Gerry Livingstone. Those who know Shetland will know that there is a considerable distance between the airport – possibly the only suitable place for a landing strip on the islands – and the capital, Lerwick. It is there that I am to meet up with my colleague, Bishop Bruce Cameron, of the Scottish Episcopal Church, who bears the title of Aberdeen and Orkney.

The Catholic church in Kirkwall, St Margaret's, is named after Queen Margaret, the saintly wife of Malcolm Canmore and not the so-called Maid of Norway. The latter's untimely death threw Scotland into a dynastic turmoil, though the Northern Isles, her dowry, were to be united thereafter to the Scottish crown.

The Episcopal church where we gather for an inter-church service is dedicated to St Magnus, the Norse Earl of Orkney who was murdered by his co-earl one fateful Easter during a parley for peace on the Isle of Egilsay.

I have been invited to preach. My sermon captures something of the spirit of the moment and reflects some of the criticism that Bishop Bruce and I have received from certain sections of the press – not that we took them too seriously!

'Just what,' asked the *Tablet*'s Notebook, 'is the Archbishop-elect of Glasgow up to, taking part in a raucous Viking festival in the Shetlands?'

I have been helped in my answer by noting that the origins of the festival are in the ancient Festival of Yule, which the Vikings held to celebrate the birth of the sun. The Romans had a similar festival, of Sol Invictus, the unconquered sun. And guess what the Christians did? They turned it into their own festival of Christmas! We still celebrate Christmas masses at midnight, dawn and mid-day in the Catholic Church – the texts of which reflect the theme of the triumph of light over darkness.

In Shetland, there's no worshipping of pagan gods, only a remembering of things past and Norse – vague and inchoate and yet clear enough in symbolic meaning. This festival is a jettisoning of the past and a looking forward in hope to the future. In Italy, the New Year is marked by throwing out, even dangerously from upper windows, old furniture and no-longer needed household items – mercifully to be uplifted before the night is over by the industrious garbage removers. In Shetland, all is consumed by fire – and what a bonfire it is!

Tuesday, 29 January

Today starts with a BBC reporter and I visiting the home of the guiser jarl, the chosen leader of the squad of Norsemen and leader of the celebrations. It is 7 a.m. when I am ushered into his front room by his douce wife. And, though I am surrounded by implements of war, there is an atmosphere of complete homeliness and friendliness that belies any sense of threatening violence!

The guiser jarl himself appears in his T-shirt and boxer shorts and, while the interview is going on, with cables all over the place, he starts to dress himself in the magnificent costume, newly designed each year, of the squad he is leading. We leave when he is in tunic and great furry leggings and we promise to meet later – as, indeed, we do!

There is a procession through the town – children from the primary schools being well marshalled by their teachers. All want to see the boat – a replica galley that will eventually be consumed by the great fire of the evening. We end up at the town hall where Bishop Bruce and I are given places of honour. The Convenor of the Council welcomes the guests and introduces the guiser jarl and his men, all of whom are given appropriate refreshment – ourselves included.

Of course, there are the inevitable photographs posed by the press. For one such shot I stand beside the guiser jarl holding his shield. A sharp photographer quickly swaps this for the axe and I am then taken next to a shielded jarl with an axe in my hand. Such is my naïvety. I wait for the day that the photograph is published over some sort of heading like 'Bishop axes 100 parishes' or 'Archbishop axes 20 schools in education review'!

The main procession takes place that evening when it is pitch dark. Around a thousand people take part, all with lighted flambeaux and marching to music – indeed, to a haunting hymn-like melody – eventually passing right next to our church and presbytery, from which we get the most marvellous view of the proceedings.

We join the crowds, appropriately fortified internally with the aid of spirits and externally with the aid of woollens. Behind the Vikings in their colourful costumes, which could almost find a place in Verdi's *Aida*, are others dressed as teddy bears, Winnie the Poohs and Mickey Mouses – or should that be Mickey Mice? All ye pagan gods where are you!

It is, despite all such incongruities, a marvellous spectacle and it reminds me of what the Easter liturgy should be. We carry our little votive candles and huddle in our churches from the cold blasts. In Shetland, they carry flambeaux and brave the elements. But the symbolism is the same – dispelling the darkness of the night with the brightness of the day. For us, the day star is Christ who dawned for us from on high and at whose resurrection the world was flooded with light. I reflect some of these thoughts in my sermon at the ecumenical service at St Magnus'.

'Up-Helly-Aa is a festival,' I tell a reporter. 'Why shouldn't bishops – and other Christians – enter into the spirit of it?' Perhaps I should have avoided the word 'spirit'! But the Christian who wishes to change the world must enter it, not flee from it (though there is a place for the occasional hermit occupying, with prayer, the more hidden corners)! The great Pastoral Constitution of the Second Vatican Council on the Church in the Modern world begins with these words:

> The joys and the hopes, the griefs and the anxieties of the men
> [and women] of this age, especially those who are poor or in any
> way affected, these too are the joys and hopes, the griefs and
> anxieties of the followers of Christ. Indeed nothing genuinely
> human fails to raise an echo in their hearts. United in Christ they
> are led by the Holy Spirit in their journey to their Father's
> Kingdom, and they have welcomed the news of salvation which
> is meant for everyone. That is why this community realises that it
> is truly and intimately linked with mankind and its history.

United in Christ . . . led by the Holy Spirit . . . [a community] linked with mankind . . . We are speaking of the Church, and we are recognising that what unites us is Christ – his Holy Spirit – our common humanity and our mission. And yet we are divided.

The ecumenical movement is the work of the Spirit making us ache to recover what has been lost. If the words *'Gaudium et Spes'* (Joy and Hope) are relevant to our cause – and I think they are – they offer us a few aims.

United in Christ they are *led by the Holy Spirit*. The aim directs us to focus on Christ – to search for his will – to seek his truth – led by the spirit – in prayer. 'Prayer,' said the Second Vatican Council, is 'the soul of the ecumenical movement.' We need to reflect and pray together – regularly.

A community linked with mankind. The aim here is to form bonds of friendship, understanding and mutual service. *Ad intra* – within the body of the disciples. Any means to foster such friendship among us must be encouraged – which is why a shared social calendar is so important, I think. *Ad extra* – towards the broader community – where the already existing bond is that of our humanity – to serve it in love.

I would love to think we could show a common face and go hand-in-hand. Quoting from St Paul to the Ephesians, 'In a word, as God's dear children, you must be like him. Live in love as Christ loved you and gave himself up on your behalf, an offering and sacrifice whose fragrance is pleasing to God' (Eph. 5: 1–2).

Already the theme of my installation sermon is beginning to form. Over the next few weeks it will take shape.

Thursday, 31 January

I returned from Shetland on Wednesday, only to leave this morning on the 6.41 a.m. plane in order to be in London for a meeting of the Presidents of Churches Together in Britain and Ireland. From a pagan festival to a Christian coven!

There are five of us elected to reflect, as far as possible, the geographical and ecclesiastical spread of the Churches in Britain and Ireland: myself, Rt Rev. John Neil, from the Church of Ireland, Rev. Nezlin Sterling, of the New Testament Assembly, and Sister Eluned Williams, from Wales and representing Methodism. The recently appointed General Secretary, Rev. David Goodbourn, considers it important to bring us together so that he can plot the road ahead.

February

Friday, 1 February

I'm back in Aberdeen to be interviewed by the BBC for the Gary Robertson show. At night I dine at Chanonry Lodge with other guests of the Principal of the University, Prof. Duncan Rice and his wife, Susan. On reflection, this plethora of events gives me great opportunity so soon after the announcement to receive the greetings and affection of friends and to respond to their inevitable question: 'How do you feel about it?'

Saturday, 2 February

It is back to 'auld clothes and porridge' – haggis actually – at the Cathedral Hall today for a delayed Burns Supper when I give the loyal toast – sorry, the 'Address to the Haggis'! Great stuff – I mean the haggis! Enough!!

Monday, 4 February

The round of press appointments continues apace. This morning it is the *Sunday Times*, this afternoon, *The Sunday Post*. Tomorrow there's a photo call, on Thursday a meeting in Edinburgh with *The Sunday Herald*, on Friday I'm doing an STV programme in Glasgow and so it goes on. I seem to be here there and everywhere. Meanwhile, preparations are continuing for my installation in Glasgow. From the beginning, my eye had alighted on the Feast of the Chair of St Peter, marked throughout the Catholic world each 22 February, as a suitable date for my induction as the new archbishop.

This feast is a mark of devotion towards the bishopric and the Bishop of Rome, connected, as it is historically and theologically, with the bishopric of Peter, to whom Christ had promised to give 'the keys of the Kingdom of Heaven'. It also falls within the time limit during which a new bishop, already consecrated, has to take up his appointment and is a day on which the apostolic nuncio is able to be present and I very much wish that he is. And so preparations start for the great day.

I have also wished, from the beginning, that the induction should be ecumenical in character – welcoming to representatives of other traditions – and so provide an opportunity for an exchange of greetings between the archdiocese and city of Glasgow and other national and local government representatives. I, therefore, suggest that the induction should take place not at a mass but at a service of prayer on 21 February, the eve of the Feast of the Chair of St Peter. It will be followed the next day by a mass that will be attended by the clergy of the archdiocese and representatives from each of the parishes. This will be more of a family occasion. The limited space at St Andrew's Cathedral makes this arrangement more logistically sound.

However, my reasons are not immediately understood and there is some pressure on me to consider having the mass first on the Feast of the Chair of St Peter and an ecumenical service on the following Sunday. I have resisted this and, at the end of the day, I am confident that my original plan will succeed.

Tuesday, 5 February – Wednesday, 6 February
I'm on my travels again – this time to Welwyn Garden City for a meeting of the Focolare Movement. This movement has, as its charism, the fostering of ecumenical spirituality and the bishops present are drawn from the Anglican and Catholic Churches.

Thursday, 7 February
I am a guest of the European Commission at Edinburgh's Balmoral Hotel. The company is excellent and discussion focuses on how institutions other than government can help facilitate a better understanding of the idea of European integration. We talk about what Britain's attitude should be to a deepening of its relationship with the European Union and a possible conversion to the Euro. I get the penultimate word and remind my table guests that the

architects of the European Union were inspired by a vision of a consolidated Europe on the path to prosperity and peace, of which it could then be an instrument for the rest of the developing world.

Friday, 8 February

I'm in Glasgow for the STV interview. This one had been planned before I was appointed and is for their *Eye-to-Eye* series. The interviewer is known to me in advance – Peter Cassidy. He is a good sort. I also have my media 'minders' Tom Cooney, Communications Officer for the Aberdeen Diocese, and Ronnie Convery, the Archdiocesan Director of Communications, with me for moral support!

Following on from yesterday's conversation, I discuss, with Ronnie, the idea of an article for the *Sunday Herald* on the issue of Europe. He is enthusiastic and we agree to prepare something on this subject. I have been offered this opportunity to write after speaking to the editor about an article printed in last week's edition which suggested I was soft on paedophile priests – an accusation that has no foundation in fact since, in my twenty-five years as bishop in Aberdeen, I was fortunate in not having had to deal with any such charges against a priest of the diocese.

The article made reference to the trial of Sister Marie Docherty of the Sisters of Nazareth in Aberdeen who was not found guilty of any of the initial twenty-six charges brought against her but, rather, of four reduced charges of 'unnatural behaviour' – for instance, throwing dirty linen at a child. To offer some balance to the coverage of the case, I said at the time of the trial that we should not lose sight of the fact that great good was done by the Sisters of Nazareth in caring competently and appropriately for many thousands of children over the years. I also pointed out that not a single charge of sexual abuse had been made against Sister Marie or any of her companions within the order.

Of course, I have no wish to minimise, in any way, the gravity of any accusation of abuse. No abuse, physical or sexual, should have a place – any place – within the Catholic Church. Both are aberrations and contrary to a tradition that has, perhaps, been best expressed by two saints associated with the care of the young. St John Bosco, founder of the Salesian homes for boys throughout the world, wrote:

> There must be no hostility in our minds, no contempt in our eyes, no insult on our lips . . . They are our sons, and so in correcting their mistakes we must lay aside all anger and restrain it so firmly that it is extinguished entirely. (*Epistolario, Torino* 4: 201–3)

St Angela Merici, founder of the Ursuline institutes for girls, wrote:

> I beg you, strive to draw them by love, modesty and charity, and not by pride and harshness. Be sincerely kind to every one . . . you are also to exercise pleasantness towards all, taking great care that what you have commanded may never be done by reason of force. (*Spiritual Testimony*, 1540)

I meet other members of the archdiocesan staff with a view to the arrangements for my installation.

Sunday, 10 February

Yesterday I attended a luncheon at Aberdeen's Town House for the Rt Rev. John Miller, the Moderator of the General Assembly of the Church of Scotland. He referred to me very warmly this morning (in fact, he referred to both me and the pope, in that order!) at King's College Chapel during his sermon for Aberdeen University's Founders' Day. In 1495 the foundation had been a sort of conspiracy between a Bishop of Aberdeen, William Elphinstone, and a pope, Alexander VI, supported by King James IV.

John's ecumenical warmth strongly contrasts with the very different spirit that was once prevalent even in the fields of academia and manifested even in such trivial matters as the omission of the name of Alexander VI from the list of benefactors of the University of Aberdeen. One of my achievements in this regard was to have Alexander VI's name added to this list when solemnly read out each year by the Principal on Founder's Day.

Tuesday, 12 February

A sad interlude amid these generally happy days. My vicar general of many years, Mgr John Provost Copland – a son of the Banffshire soil and as sound and fruitful as the land from which he came – has died. He is buried today at Tombae after mass at St Thomas', Keith, at which I preside. A Keith 'loon', Fr Andrew Mann, gives the moving homily. It seems, in some ways, a fitting time for us to part but one that is nonetheless saddening – the end of an era. I leave his grave with a deep sense of loss – of a man, of a dying culture, of a depopulating community in the Braes of Glenlivet.

Wednesday, 13 February

Today is Ash Wednesday and the beginning of Lent, a season that will start for me in Aberdeen and end in Glasgow. I say mass for the children of St Joseph's School and am presented with a beautiful memento from them. It comes in the form of a statue of St Joseph and the child Jesus in bronze resin by Anne Davidson – the same sculptor who modelled the impressive figure of the Soweto woman and child which stands with her back (as perhaps well she might) to Edinburgh's Sheraton Hotel and facing (perhaps more appropriately) the Usher Hall. There is, after all, more hope of compassion through art than through luxury.

Friday, 15 February

I inscribe, at St Mary's Cathedral, for the last time as bishop, the names of the new catechumens – those preparing for baptism and the profession of the Catholic faith at the Easter vigil.

Saturday, 16 February

This is my last confirmation of the children in the diocese, at St Margaret's, Forres. In nearly twenty-five years up and down its lovely land, I have confirmed virtually every Catholic child who has received the sacrament. Such confirmation occasions have been among the happiest and, I believe, most fruitful exercises of my ministry as a bishop. Parents, grandparents, friends and parishioners have stood in support of these lovely twelve- and thirteen-year-olds as they professed the faith handed on to them. They have been signed with the cross in the oil of chrism as a mark of their readiness to face the future with Christian courage.

Chrism sounds like 'charisma' and, in a way, the two are related since it is a sign of grace from above.

Sunday, 17 February

From Forres, I go on to Inverness, capital of the Highlands, with its own distinctive character both as a civic community and as a church. It is marked by that gentleness and piety which we associate with the best of Highland folk, though those chief characteristics can give way to a narrowness of mind, inbred in small communities, that can shut doors to other folk and other faiths, notoriously on the Sabbath. On the other hand, we can admire the tenacity of some such church communities which have held on to their traditional faith over the years. Can we still hear, in the extraordinary psalm tones of the Free Presbyterians, echoes of the early Church?

It was in monks' cells, perched on precipitous crags and on remote but lovely islands that the Gospels were stored and the faith preserved during the darkest days of barbarism in Europe. These were days when the breaches in the old Roman order, not at first sympathetic to Christianity, were so many as to leave the former centres of European civilisation exposed on every side to Vandals, Goths and Huns – the very names of which still cause a slight frisson of terror in our consciousness. (In Glasgow patois, the idea of the archbishop being afraid of the Huns might mean something quite different – or so I'm told!) However, in the ravaged land of that old order, as in a ploughed field, the seeds of a new Christian civilisation were sown by Celtic missionaries. These flowered and came to fruition in a marvellous new order, marked by monasteries, ennobled by cathedrals and enriched by seats of learning. All over the continent of Europe we see signs of this missionary activity.

In Scotland, places of learning survived but none of the abbeys and few of the cathedrals did. A new breed of vandals crossed the land in the wake of religious upheaval and civil strife in the sixteenth century. And it was not only buildings but also a burgeoning renaissance musical tradition and fine art that fell victim to the changes.

Today our society is undergoing other changes and the enemy, in whatever guise it might take – secularism, atheism or consumerism – uses a cultural weapon which calls for the equipping of the Christian with the armour of the spirit so elegantly described by St Paul: 'Put on the armour of faith . . .' (Romans 13: 14).

It is funny how the mention of a place can conjure up such thoughts. I mean, Inverness, which according to tradition received the faith from St Columba himself, travelling up the Highland glens with his companions and chasing away, for the time being at any rate, a monster that was terrorising the inhabitants. (Nessie, by any chance?)

I am fond of Inverness, the place where my grandparents married and my father was born. I have the shield of Inverness, containing the image of the crucified Christ, adorning the chalice which my mother's family gave me on my ordination day, 6 October 1958, at San Marcello al Corso in Rome.

I'm here today for the last time as bishop-administrator and receive a warm welcome from my devoted colleague and friend, Mgr Robert McDonald, parish priest of St Mary's, Inverness, and Denny, the Highlands. As I did a few days earlier at St Mary's Cathedral, I inscribe, in what is called the 'Book of the Elect', the names of those adult converts who are seeking membership of the Catholic Church – through baptism, a profession of faith, confirmation and communion – at the Easter vigil. Afterwards I stand at the end of the aisle by the open door which looks on to the swiftly flowing River Ness to bid goodbye to the parishioners. Over the years, I have come to know them well – their good wishes ring in my ears for the rest of the day. It is not without sadness that I depart, though I am to return in the autumn to the newly designated city for the third diocesan celebration of my silver jubilee as bishop.

I drive back to Aberdeen by way of Elgin and stop off for tea at Greyfriars, once a ruined Franciscan friary and subsequently renovated, as was the nearby Benedictine Abbey of Pluscarden, through the generosity of the third Marquis of Bute. Today Greyfriars is the Convent of the Sisters of Mercy, whose influence on my early years was profound and whose subsequent hospitality has been as enduring. You can guess at the affection with which I am sent on my way, to Glasgow, with a framed photograph of the convent and other mementoes.

The *Sunday Herald* has taken up our offer of an article on Europe and publish it today. Here is the text.

In the few short weeks since the announcement of my appointment as Archbishop of Glasgow, the one question which recurs in almost every interview is: 'What are you going to do about sectarianism?' The truth, of course, is that neither I nor, I suspect, any other single individual can hope to solve a problem which has deep historical roots. On the day my appointment was made public I stated, in a slightly tongue-in-cheek manner, that I came as 'an innocent' from the north-east. It is not completely true to say that my native diocese is a bigotry-free zone. Once, as an uninvited guest, I attended public meetings in Wick and Thurso called by a religious group to denounce the wickedness of the Catholic Church. I doubt whether they would happen today.

However, it is true that the issue of sectarianism is now, more than ever, at the forefront of my mind. Especially after a recent dinner where my table companions were consular representatives, captains of industry, bankers, representatives from the worlds of politics and religion, and a couple of ministers of state. We were hosted by a member of the European Commission and the discussion focused on British attitudes to the European Union. It occurred to me that there is a link between the issues of sectarianism and European integration. In both cases one could discern a mentality primarily focused on protecting narrow interests; a failure to respond to the opportunities to build larger communities of support and affection.

So how can this mentality be tackled most effectively at both local and international level? Of course, the fundamental condition for any progress is a willingness to sit down and engage in dialogue. This approach has produced significant results in the on-going discussion between the Catholic Church and other Christian bodies, culminating most recently in the joint declaration of understanding between Catholics and Lutherans on the question of justification (a theological equivalent of the Great War).

We must also remember the enormous achievement of the EU's founding fathers: the French economist, Jean Monnet, and Premier Robert Schuman, West German Chancellor, Konrad Adenauer, and Italian Premier, Alcide de Gasperi. These were men of vision and faith. They accomplished what many in the early 1950s believed impossible; they put in place structures which ensured a new era of peaceful co-operation between nations which had been at war for almost as long as they had been in existence.

Peace within the borders of what has become the EU is too often overlooked. For fifty years the Catholic Church has accompanied the process of greater European interdependence with encouragement. This year Pope John Paul said: 'Among reasons for satisfaction, one must mention the progressive unification of Europe, recently symbolised by the adoption of a single currency by twelve countries. This is a decisive step in the long history of this continent.'

I regret that in our own country there has been a lamentable lack of interest in our common European inheritance. Perhaps the closed-minded bigotry which demeans many people in their attitude to religion is, alas, also present in the aggressively anti-European stance adopted by some politicians and commentators. All too often the fine work of dialogue and harmonisation, work which aims to support the common good of all at a European level, is minimised and despised by those who prefer parochial safety to the vulnerable adventure of interdependence.

Sections of the press let us down. Lurid tabloid headlines about Brussels's rulings on bananas or Eurodiktats on chocolate coarsen our culture, depress the standard of debate and debase our country's standing in Europe. The Catholic Church has no truck with such petty isolationism. It proclaims a message of common relevance to every man, woman and child in Europe and beyond.

Although I am a great supporter of closer European integration, I must sound a note of caution. In the head-long rush for more effective trade rules and early tax harmonisation, we are in danger of falling into two traps. On the one hand lies a culture of consumption, dislocated from any system of values and, on the other, a continent-wide isolationism; a kind of European 'I'm all right Jack' mentality. And this at a time when economic disparity is an ever-widening chasm between north and south, the first and third worlds. European integration was not meant as an end in itself, but as a means to an end, namely that of promoting a more just, stable and peaceful continent, which could in turn contribute to a better world.

Given that the expediency of a constitution for the EU has recently been questioned, it is essential to make increasingly explicit the goals of European unification and the values on which it must rest.

I am concerned, therefore, that no mention was made of communities of religious believers among the partners who are to contribute to the reflection on the 'convention' instituted at the Laeken Summit last December. In the words of Pope John Paul,

'The marginalisation of religions, which have contributed and
continue to contribute to the culture and humanism of which
Europe is legitimately proud, strikes me as both an injustice and
an error of perspective.' Any attempt to build a European
identity among the nations of the old continent is doomed to
failure if it does not take into account the history of the continent
and the religious sense of its people.

We have come a long way since the intellectual, Hilaire Belloc,
exclaimed, 'Europe is the faith and the faith is Europe' – meaning
the Catholic faith. I suspect his assertion, memorable though it is,
was based on wishful thinking. Today, Europe is a melting pot of
100 languages and almost as many religions and faith traditions.
Those traditions must be recognised in any new European
constitution.

At the same time, Europe cannot set itself up as an exclusive
club, unwilling to share the benefits of unity with others from the
East and ultimately with the poorer nations of the South. Such a
Europe would be unworthy of its own origins. Expansion of the
EU is a *sine qua non* [an indispensable condition] if it is to
continue to enjoy the support of the Church. I recall very well
the appeal of John Paul II in Gniezno, Poland, in 1997 to
European leaders: 'May they not leave any nation, not even the
weakest, outside the group they are building.'

Which takes me back to sectarianism and the lessons that we
can draw from the model of European integration. In the first
place, I see the need for bravery on the part of community
leaders. We need men and women at a local level with something
of the vision and determination of Schuman and De Gasperi,
prepared to say what needs to be said and labour tirelessly for
greater understanding.

Secondly, I see the need for some serious soul-searching
among all faith traditions. We need to have the courage to ask
ourselves whether we have, explicitly or implicitly, encouraged
hostility towards those of other faiths, remembering that sins of
omission can be just as serious as sins of commission. I recall the

powerful words of my predecessor when he expressed his 'shame' as Archbishop of Glasgow at the treatment meted out to asylum-seekers by some of our fellow citizens.

Thirdly, I see the need for the rebirth of a sense of universal brotherhood, capable of looking beyond name, ethnic origin, football scarves and skin colour. Our common humanity is the fundamental ground of unity; the common fatherhood of God is its source and guarantee.

As a Christian, I believe that the effect of Christ's death and resurrection is to unite all of humanity in renewed creation. As Jesus himself put it, 'When I am lifted up I shall draw all to myself' (John 12: 32). The cross and the resurrection should be the source of communion and fraternity. It is a scandal, in the fullest sense of that word, that those who call themselves Christian turn religion into an excuse for hatred, injustice and violence.

Finally, I believe we can learn from the European experience that no effort to tackle sectarianism and division can succeed by ignoring the spiritual side of our nature. It cannot be done without vision.

If perverted, religion must share some of the blame for causing the problems of bigotry, then authentic religion must play its part in solving them. The French philosopher, Montesquieu, quipped in one of his letters: 'No Kingdom has ever suffered as many civil wars as Christ's.'

If my period of service as archbishop can contribute to the breaking-down of just some of the misunderstandings, enmities and prejudices that have disfigured the noble face of Glasgow, then I shall be content. And it will no doubt be evident from what I have written above that my desire to promote community harmonisation is drafted on a larger canvas.

Tuesday, 19 February

The article in last week's *Sunday Herald* produced conflicting responses. Some were warmly supportive, including one from 10

Downing Street, and some highly critical, in particular *The Scotsman*, whose comments in their leading article yesterday were so over the top that I found myself, perhaps for the first time, laughing off criticism which had invalidated itself by its intemperate nature.

Wednesday, 20 February

This is my last day as bishop-administrator of the diocese and not inappropriately, in a way, it is mainly taken up with a meeting of the diocesan finance committee.

It is strange to be back in Aberdeen, of which I am still in charge but now as 'administrator' rather than 'bishop' – a curious position to be in as the only effective difference is that I now have to obtain the advice or permission of the College of Consultors (a group of senior priests of the diocese) to act in certain more important matters, particularly to do with finance.

In anticipation of this meeting, I have managed to obtain the consent of the College to an important proposal. It is to ensure that a significant bequest – which had been made to the Diocese of Aberdeen by a former parishioner of the cathedral and invested on the cathedral's behalf – should be realised in part, to allow a major project to be undertaken. The project, to which the Finance Committee agreed, involves the extension of the cathedral rooms in the remaining space at the south side of the building.

This project has been taking shape ever since it became obvious that better kitchen space should be provided for the halls. One thing led to another . . . I am very pleased to be able, as my last administrative act, to see a hall now being provided to serve the social needs of the parish and also those of the diocese on occasions when the cathedral comes into its own as the centre of its activity. In my mind, the next likely occasion will be the consecration of my successor as bishop.

We have the usual long agenda culminating in a happy social event – a meal and presentation of a painting to Mrs Joyce Simpson, who has served for nearly two decades as financial adviser and minute secretary to the committee. What I haven't bargained for is the presentation to me of a coloured print by Donald M. Shearer of Aberdeen Harbour. I'm not going to be allowed to forget my time here!

Thursday, 21 February

A haze of glorious memories fills today. Some of them will be forever fixed, I suspect, by the photographers covering the occasion of my taking canonical possession of St Andrew's Cathedral this evening.

The day starts in Aberdeen with mass in the oratory served by the faithful Sister Molly. I present her with a little china bird. It was precious to me for sentimental reasons since I had given it to my mother on her eightieth birthday. I'm sure Sister Molly will treasure it and she certainly deserves to have it.

My other goodbyes are equally poignant – to my faithful PA, Irene Melling, and the Diocesan Secretary, Joyce Webster, though I know both will be at my installation in Glasgow, and to Anne McDonald, my caring daily housekeeper whose sandwiches fortify me on my journey.

I originally thought of going by train but the large number of cases I have to carry and the other advantages of the car result in me driving myself to my new responsibilities in Glasgow. It is a wretched day weather-wise, cold, wet and blustery. By evening there is sleet, all too similar to the day I was ordained a bishop nearly twenty-five years ago – though that had been in May! Stormy days ahead? Hopefully not!

As I approach the turn-off from the M8 marked 'Glasgow Cathedral', I am strongly tempted to take it. I could go there and pray on St Mungo's tomb. I am conscious – and, if I had not been, constant reference to the fact would have made me so – that I was succeeding the saint as bishop in this place. There are a thousand years between his death and that of the last pre-Reformation Archbishop of Glasgow, Archbishop James Beaton, who died in Paris in 1603. He had wisely fled there with the treasury and archives of his cathedral. Not for him the ignominious death by hanging of his fellow Archbishop of St Andrews, John Hamilton, whom the Reformers hanged in his mass vestments – despite the fact that this man had tried, all too late, to reform the Church from within.

But such thoughts are not uppermost in my mind, mercifully, this rainy afternoon as I drive over the Kingston Bridge and find myself eventually at 40 Newlands Road, the late Cardinal's residence which is to be my new home. Mrs Mac (Isobel McInnes), Cardinal Tom's devoted housekeeper, welcomes me warmly.

I am ready when the car comes to collect me later that day, though I must admit my heart sinks somewhat when I see the stretch limousine. Archbishop James Scanlan, one of my predecessors, immediately comes to mind. He was publicly criticised – at a time when such criticism was rarely heard – for the large car by which he made his presence known throughout the city. It transpired that it had been given to him by his sister but this did nothing to take away the opprobrium. Perhaps he felt the time had come for him to be seen about his pastoral visits in the city. My second thought is that the car looks rather like a hearse – a thought that is not dispelled when I discover that it belongs to an undertaker's firm!

However, the car has been most generously put at my disposal for the day and there is nothing for it but to get in and be whisked away to the cathedral and the next door curial offices where I am to rest. I disembark speedily, not only for reasons of embarrassment but also to avoid the increasingly wintry wind!

I get dressed in the choir dress of a bishop – namely, a purple or magenta soutane with sash, over which I wear a surplice made of linen and lace which was given to me by my Italian relatives at my ordination as a priest in Rome so many years before. Over this a bishop normally wears a mozzetta – a small cape which originally had a hood, this latter element having been dispensed with in recent years. Under the leadership of Gerry Byrne, the six seminarians of the archdiocese have decided to give me something and I suggest a new mozzetta. The Roman students had brought it back with them this very day and are now in the foyer of the office ready to give it to me. I am photographed putting it on with their help.

Mgr Peter Smith lines up all those who are to join the procession, among whom are the two suffragan bishops, Bishop Joe Devine of Motherwell and Bishop John Mone of Paisley, along with Pablo Puente, the apostolic nuncio, who carries in his hand the bull of appointment. When all is ready, we set off, briskly crossing the small courtyard between the offices and the cathedral and glad to get out of the blustery wind and sleet into the warmth of the cathedral foyer.

What a contrast to the dark and dismal weather outside. In the porch are assembled the canons with their provost at their head. There is a very short but meaningful ceremony for a bishop entering his cathedral church. He is offered the crucifix to kiss and then given a basin of holy water from which he sprinkles himself and those around him. No words are spoken but glances and smiles are exchanged. To the glorious sound of organ and choir, we then process into the church.

I remember in particular kneeling alone at the steps of the sanctuary in front of the altar. If I had not already been a bishop, I would have had to prostrate myself, with all around me kneeling in supplication and the sonorous invocations to Our Lady and all the saints washing over me. But I am a bishop and I simply kneel there in silence while all stand around me, observing. It is thoughtful of the Master of Ceremonies, my Chancellor Mgr Peter Smith, to suggest this otherwise I would have gone straight to the cathedra, or bishop's chair, to take possession of it.

This moment is significant. I am before the altar, the symbol of Christ's sacrifice. I am giving myself to a task to which I believe He is calling me: 'Come follow me!' Inchoate prayers, best summed up by 'Help me, Lord', arise from deep within me but I remain all too conscious that all eyes are on me – and conscious too that my glasses have completely steamed up and I can't see a thing!

Not a very appropriate metaphor to describe the moment. But

the moment is nonetheless precious. With spectacles removed and carefully held along with the awkward biretta – the purple hat worn on such occasions – I eventually get to my feet and make my way towards the throne which has been unoccupied since the death of Cardinal Winning.

No one leads me to the chair, neither metropolitan – I am he – nor my fellow bishops. I am there by 'the grace of God and the favour of the Apostolic See', to use the time-honoured formula. The hand that leads and upholds me is the same that had been extended to Peter as he felt himself sinking into the waves. It is Peter's successor who now confirms me in my office. His letter is read out in the distinctively Spanish accent of the apostolic nuncio, Archbishop Pablo Puente.

During the reading I have an opportunity to take in the scene. To my right and left are the two suffragan bishops and, beyond them in the sanctuary, members of the cathedral chapter and other representatives of the clergy. Beyond are the distinguished guests, among whom I recognise the Lord and Lady Provost of Glasgow, Alex and Maureen Mosson, the First Minister of the Scottish Parliament and his wife, Jack and Bridget McConnell, the Secretary of State for Scotland, Helen Liddell and her husband, the leader of the SNP, John Swinney, David Davidson MSP, from the Scottish Conservatives, and representatives from the universities and the worlds of the arts, business, sport and press. The attendance of all these civic dignitaries underlines the necessary relationship between Church and state – a theme I develope in my homily. I am able to notice too that my brother-in-law has safely arrived. Unfortunately, my sister is not present because of ill health, though I see my nephew, John, and, to my very great pleasure, my cousin from Italy, Agostino Caproni, along with the parish priest of my family's home town of Barga, Mgr Piero Giannini.

Here, for the record, is the homily I preached.

Dear friends, members of the archdiocese and honoured guests,
    I am very conscious that my first words to you from this chair

will be scrutinised and analysed rather more profoundly than some future homilies I may preach. And it is right that it should be so.

Those who examine the life and work of Pope John Paul II often refer to his first words spoken on the balcony of St Peter's Basilica on the night of his election. His phrase 'do not be afraid' has been a kind of leitmotiv running through the subsequent two-and-a-half decades of his service as successor of St Peter.

In spite of my limitations, I have been called to be the Archbishop and Metropolitan of this great See of Glasgow, which is proud to bear the historic title *Specialis Filia Romanae Ecclesiae*, 'Special Daughter of the Roman Church'. It seemed particularly appropriate, therefore, to have my installation on the Feast of the Chair of St Peter, an ancient commemoration which reminds our Catholic people of the living links of our faith with St Peter and the Apostles, mediated through their successors.

For like reason, it is natural that I should look to St Peter for a word of direction and encouragement and I find it in the first of his two letters contained in the canon of scripture. From Rome shortly before his death under Nero, he writes a sort of summary of the Christian faith and of the duties, which stem from it relative to God, to fellow members of the Church and to the wider community under its civic leaders. First of all he addresses the community of faith itself, underlining its vocation: 'You are a chosen race, a community of priest-kings, a consecrated nation, a people God has made his own to proclaim his wonders, for he called you from your darkness to his own wonderful light' (1 Pet. 2: 9).

First of all I want to greet you, my brothers and sisters of the Catholic faith, represented here by both clergy and laity. I embrace you with a bishop's love.

St Peter sees the vocation of each Christian community as that of following Christ in service of the human family of which it is part. He instructs us:

FEBRUARY

For the Lord's sake, respect all human authority: God wants you to do good so that you may silence those fools who ignorantly criticise you. Behave as free people but do not speak of freedom as a licence for vice; you are free men and God's servants. Reverence each person, love your brothers and sisters, fear God and show respect to the emperor. (1 Pet. 2: 13–17)

Dear Friends, I asked that this evening's celebration should be one at which I might meet representatives of all sections of Glasgow's civic, cultural and religious life. It would thus provide me with an opportunity of paying my respects to all sections of the community and of stretching out the hand of friendship.

This hand of friendship is extended first of all to our fellow Christians of other traditions and then to those of other faith communities whose contribution to the life of this city is so critical to its continuing development.

It is extended also to the members of all those institutions which you represent: to government, national and local; to law; to education and commerce; to industry and the arts; to sport, entertainment and to the media of communication. I would like to reflect a little on the nature and character of this friendship, based, as it is, upon our common humanity and shared experience. It is exercised in respectful dialogue.

There was for us Catholics in 1965 an important day when the late Pope Paul VI signed the Second Vatican Council's Constitution on the Church in the Modern World, *Gaudium et Spes* – joy and hope. The opening words of that text have become a kind of mission statement of the modern Catholic Church, and I borrow from it quite unashamedly to describe my own personal resolution as the leader of this community:

The joys and the hopes, the griefs and the anxieties of the men [and women] of this age, especially those who are poor or in any way afflicted, these too are the joys and hopes, the griefs and the anxieties of the followers of Christ (*GS* 1).

61

I want to say that the Church no longer stands at a critical distance from the society which it addresses. It is not a citadel on a hill or a fortified ghetto. It is a Church at the heart of the city, at the heart of the world; a Church passionately in love with humanity.

In the same constitution we read:

> To carry out [its] task, the Church has always had the duty of scrutinising the signs of the times – [a phrase much loved by my predecessor] and of interpreting them in the light of the Gospel. Thus, in language intelligible to each generation, she can respond to the perennial questions which men ask about this present life and the life to come, and about the relation-ship of the one to the other. We must therefore recognise and understand the world in which we live, its expectations, its longings, and its often dramatic characteristics. (GS 4)

Though this document was written some thirty-five years ago, its assessment is still relevant:

> Today, the human race is passing through a new stage of its history. Profound and rapid changes are spreading by degrees around the whole world. Triggered by the intelligence and creative energies of man, these changes recoil upon him, on his decisions and desires, both individual and collective, and upon his manner of thinking and acting with respect to things and people. (ibid.)

The authors of this document recognised that: 'Advances in biology, psychology, and the social sciences not only bring men hope of improved self-knowledge, but, in conjunction with technical methods, they are also helping men to exert direct influence on the life of social groups' (GS 5). Inevitably, 'there has arisen a new series of problems, a series as important as can be, calling for new efforts of analysis and synthesis' (ibid.).

I hope we will be allowed to make our own contribution to these analyses and syntheses. I would like to think that the voice of the Church, articulated through its leaders, will not be disregarded as a voice from the distant past, as if the past had no relevance to the present but is heard/heeded as a witness to a tradition of wisdom and an expertise gained over 2000 years of dealing with humanity.

There is, in fact, a long history of co-operation between the Church and the institutions of this city. Who can forget that, in 1451, the co-operative energies of King James II, Pope Nicholas V and Bishop Turnbull of Glasgow resulted in the establishment of the city's first university? Modelled on the University of Bologna, Glasgow was, and has remained, a university in the great European tradition. The university, which is such a jewel in the city's crown, was born *ex corde ecclesiae* – from the heart of the Church.

The old university and its new colleagues give the city the reputation of being a place of learning and culture, enhanced by its galleries and its vibrant companies of musicians, artists and performers, whose national programmes are directed from this city.

In more recent times, but in that same tradition of promoting learning, the Catholic Church, at considerable cost to its members, established and then entered into partnership with the state for the continuation of a system of primary and secondary education based upon Gospel values and consonant with the faith of its people. This partnership has worked well and the contribution of the Catholic schools sector to Scottish education is widely acknowledged. Does anyone seriously believe that the way to foster a united community is to deprive one section of it of its hard won achievements?

Another area of outstanding contribution from the Church throughout the centuries has been care of the most needy. From the hospices of early monastic communities to the wide range of charitable works directed towards the poorest people of Glasgow in the nineteenth and twentieth centuries, the Church has sought to fulfill the Gospel imperative of love of neighbour.

Many of the religious communities in the archdiocese were founded precisely to provide services to the poor, the homeless, the sick and the dying. Following in that tradition, Cardinal Winning established a widely respected community social services department in the 1970s.

Today the archdiocese, working in partnership with civic and national agencies, administers thirty-three social care projects. Those who benefit range from people with learning or physical disabilities; people with mental health problems; those who misuse drugs; the vulnerable elderly and the vulnerable young – of all faiths and none. Such projects are fine examples of what can be achieved for the common good, through co-operation between the Church and civil authorities.

Respect, friendship, dialogue, co-operation – these are some of the key words of this address. Indirectly they answer the question of how we are to face the challenge of residual sectarianism and bigotry which unfortunately at times still mar the face of this great city. We know there are no magic solutions to the problem. We sense that it is going to be an uphill struggle but we are convinced that, ultimately, by all sections of the community working together and the grace of God coming upon us, ancient animosities will give way to a civilisation of love.

'Do not be afraid,' said Pope John Paul II and we take comfort from his words. 'Bow down,' said St Peter, 'before the power of God so that He will raise you up at the appointed time. Place all your worries on Him since he takes care of you . . . Glory be to Him for ever and ever. Amen' (1 Pet. 5: 6, 7, 11).

Thank you all for coming this evening, my brother Bishops of the Province of Glasgow and representatives of the clergy and people of the diocese. Thank you to the representatives of the many strands which make up the community of this city. You have not only done me an honour in your attendance but you have also honoured the Church which I am now unworthily appointed to lead. I have every confidence that we can and will strive together to enable Glasgow to flourish to the glory of God and the well-being of all its citizens.

Thank you.

At the end of the ceremony I take my place at the very edge of the sanctuary and there greet, one by one, the distinguished guests. I cannot help but think that, but for my predecessor's projection of the archbishop's office on to the public stage through the power of his personality, I would not be receiving, in so public a manner, the congratulations and good wishes of so many distinguished persons, leaders of both church and state at national and civic level.

Whether I like it or not – I certainly appreciate it – I am standing in the shoes of my predecessor.

Friday, 22 February

After last night's apparently successful installation, about which the press were generally complimentary both in the words they chose and the photos they published, I do not feel diffident this morning. After all, mass will be very much a family occasion. The presence of the Speaker of the House of Commons and the Lord Provost of Glasgow will not alter that since both of them are members of the family of the Church.

The same car comes for me and I hope, once again, that not too many people will see me in it or issuing from it!

I get in early and so am able to welcome the cardinals, archbishops and bishops who have assembled for the occasion. Cardinal Cormac Murphy-O'Connor has unfortunately been prevented from attending, though he has sent a very generous message. It is, therefore, all the more impressive that two Irish cardinals, the Archbishop Emeritus of Armagh, Cahal Daly, and the Archbishop of Dublin, Desmond Connell, come and flank me in the sanctuary. Other Irish bishop friends, including the two members of the Catholic Bishops Joint Bioethics Committee, Donal Murray of Limerick and Patrick Walsh of Down and Connor, are also there, along with the Auxiliary Bishop of Down and Connor, Bishop Tony Farquhar, a very dear friend from the field of ecumenism, though how he puts up with my lack of sporting savvy, I will never know!

The Archbishop of Birmingham, Vincent Nichols, is here, his diocese having a special place in my affection as the birthplace of my mother – in every sense my second home. All my colleagues from the Bishops' Conference of Scotland are present under the leadership of the President of the Conference, Archbishop Keith Patrick O'Brien. We have been friends since he was rector of Blairs and I was the young local bishop. I have a sense that we coached one another in our respective offices.

The priests of the archdiocese are out in force and, adding to their number, are priests from Aberdeen and other friends from elsewhere. They fill a third of the cathedral, as well as the whole of the sanctuary.

Once more, under the leadership of Mgr Gerry Fitzpatrick, whom I recall as a young student in Rome, the St Mungo Singers supply the music. And we are honoured, once again, by the presence of the apostolic nuncio who, again, patiently reads out, with his distinctive Spanish accent, the papal bull of appointment.

I am wearing a magnificently embroidered vestment given to me by my former vicar general – the parish priest of Buckie, Mgr Eddie Traynor. I had admired and used it on a previous occasion and he insists that I should have it. I take it under protest, insisting that it would only be a loan and that, in due course, it will return to the parish to which it belongs. My mitre still bears the symbols of the Diocese of Aberdeen, but I have little alternative since I have tried on virtually every one that Mgr Peter keeps in a cupboard in the offices and none would fit. If I had fitted into Cardinal Tom's shoes last night, it is clear I am not going to fit into his mitre today!

After the bull of appointment is read out, I am presented with the crozier of the archdiocese, the symbol of the bishop's office as a pastor of souls. This modern and very fine piece of Scottish silver work has inscribed, round its staff, the names of the Archbishops of Glasgow and, to these, my name has been added. I am, however, somewhat taken aback by the weight of it. If a staff is intended to support you, then this crozier militates against its purpose. To process with it in your left hand while turning to right and left in the best traditional manner to bless the gathered faithful is certainly not the easiest of movements. Occasionally I feel I'm going to topple over, so heavy it is. Maybe that is a useful metaphor: the bearer of the pastoral staff, while he holds to his office, must ever be aware of his human frailty. Nonetheless, having received it, I am moved to kiss it before giving it to one of the young servers to hold.

All who came to the cathedral last night are able to take a full part in the proceedings. Michael Martin, the Speaker of the House of Commons and himself an MP for a Glasgow constituency, was unable to come yesterday but is present today at the mass. He is joined again by Alex Mosson, Lord Provost of Glasgow with his wife, Maureen. Both are men of great character who make no secret of their being active members of Glasgow parishes whenever their duties allow.

Here are the words I use in my first formal mass homily, preached to the priests and people of Glasgow.

Dear brothers and sisters in Christ

I celebrate with you today my installation as your archbishop and I do so on the Feast of the Chair of St Peter, an appropriate day for the Archdiocese of Glasgow which is proud to carry the historic title of *Specialis Filia Romanae Ecclesiae* – 'the Special Daughter of the Roman Church'. This ancient feast stands as a reminder to us of our living links of faith with St Peter and the Apostles and their successors, the pope and bishops.

It was natural that I should look to St Peter to find a word of direction and encouragement and I found it in the first of his two letters contained in the canon of scripture: 'You are a chosen race,' he says, 'a community of priest-kings, a consecrated nation, a people God has made his own to proclaim his wonders' (1 Pet. 2: 9).

St Peter urges us to live in this present world, in the midst of its society, in such a way as to confound all those who may criticise our way of life or disparage our message:

> For the Lord's sake, respect all human authority: the king as chief authority, the governors as sent by him to punish evildoers and to encourage those who do good. And God wants you to do good so that you may silence those fools who ignorantly criticise you. Behave as free people but do not speak of freedom as a licence for vice; you are free men and God's servants. Reverence each person, love your brothers and sisters, fear God and show respect to the emperor. (1 Pet. 2: 13–17)

I used this passage at last night's installation in order to express my hope that the Catholic Church in Glasgow may continue to influence, from within the society of which it is part and to seek from all those representing its various strands, their co-operation, in response to the hand of friendship extended to them.

This letter deserves our attention since it is a sort of blueprint for the Christian life left to us by the first Pope. It is an active plan of life, involving setting proper priorities, serving the common good, engaging in the apostolate, bearing witness bravely and building up the Kingdom of God in our world.

For the Christians of Glasgow, especially for laymen and women, this is a new and challenging task. We know it is no longer possible to leave the work of the Church to the clergy, to the religious, to the hierarchy and this impossibility is not due simply to a reduction in the number of priests, but to a better understanding of the role of the laity and consequently, to a

better understanding of the role of the ministerial priesthood.
The Second Vatican Council said:

The laity exercise a genuine apostolate by their activity in
bringing the Gospel and holiness to men [and women] and in
penetrating and perfecting the temporal sphere of things
through the spirit of the Gospel. In this way, their temporal
activity can openly bear witness to Christ and promote the
salvation of mankind. Since it is proper to the layman's state
in life for him to spend his days in the midst of the world and
in secular transactions, he is called by God to burn with the
Spirit of Christ and to exercise his apostolate in the world as a
kind of leaven. (Decree on the Apostolate of the Laity)

One of the most significant witnesses, and the one perhaps
needed above all in our day, is that of conjugal fidelity and
parental love. The Fathers of the Second Vatican Council said of
the apostolate of married persons and of families that it was 'of
unique importance both for the Church and civil society'. They
recalled that 'the Creator of all things established the conjugal
partnership as the beginning and basis of human society and, by
His grace, has made it a great mystery of Christ and the Church'.
We must do all we can to support marriage and the family. That
will undoubtedly be one of my main priorities.

It is now some thirty-five years since the Second Vatican
Council. The need expressed then has become ever more pressing
because of the progressive secularisation of our society and its
increasing reluctance to heed the official voice of the Church. It is
not as if that voice has not been heard. It has reverberated from
this very place, through the powerful words and witness of my
predecessor of happy memory. However, words will only be
heeded if those who speak can back them, not only with the
example of their own lives but the lives of the community they
lead.

Today, therefore, the need is greater than ever for each man and woman, baptised into the Church, to live a life of holiness, of commitment, entering into dialogue with the men and women of our time, offering to all the gifts of wisdom of the Catholic Church, while, at the same time, respecting the sanctuary of another's conscience.

We have natural allies in this task and I refer, of course, to our fellow Christians of other traditions. Our Holy Father has taught us to respect also the members of other great world religions, an increasing number of whom are found in our own city and, indeed, in our own schools.

It was in this very city, at Bellahouston in 1982, that our Holy Father invited us all to walk together 'hand in hand'. It is my intention, as your bishop, to do all I can to increase ecumenical understanding, friendship and co-operation. What we have in view is the organic unity of the Church, a unity which Christ himself gave us as the necessary sign 'that all men may believe'. Indeed, that unity was the 'glory' that He offered to His Apostles at the Last Supper as the fruit of his own passion, death and resurrection. St John reminds us that Jesus died 'to gather into one the scattered children of God' (John 11: 51). St Peter said:

This is your calling. Remember Christ who suffered for you leaving you an example so that you may follow in his way. He did not return insult for insult and, when suffering, he did not curse but put himself in the hands of God who judges justly. He went to the cross burdened with our sins so that we might die to sin and live an upright life, for by his wounds you have been healed. You were like stray sheep, but you have come back to the shepherd and guardian of your souls. (1 Pet. 2: 21–5)

It is by that humility and forbearance that we will help to overcome any residual sectarianism and bigotry which unfortunately has, all too often, marred the face of this great city. It will not be by the dismantling of our Catholic schools that bigotry will be overcome but by learning in them that necessary attitude of respect and tolerance which I am certain our teachers already aim to instill in the minds and hearts of our youngsters.

You can depend on me to defend this invaluable legacy of our forebears and to strive to ensure the highest quality of teaching and faith practiced in them.

St Peter has a message also for the shepherds:

> Shepherd the flock which God has entrusted to you, guarding it not out of obligation but willingly for God's sake; not as one looking for a reward but with a generous heart; do not lord it over those in your care, rather be an example to your flock. Then, when the Chief Shepherd appears, you will be given a crown of unfading glory. (ibid. 5: 1–4)

I take those words to heart myself.

The task of shepherding is, however, a shared one and I look forward, with pleasure and great expectation, to meeting you, my fellow shepherds and brother priests, at the earliest opportunity so that we can pray and plan together how best we can care for the lovely people committed to our charge. Without you, I can do nothing. Together we can do a very great deal.

Finally, I address the religious, to whom we, both clergy and laity, turn for inspiration and support, the inspiration of lives totally dedicated to Christ and the support of prayers offered constantly at the heart of the Church. 'This Sacred Synod,' said the Fathers of the Second Vatican Council, 'has high regard for the character of [your] life – virginal, poor, and obedient – of which Christ the Lord himself is the model. The Council places steady hope in the immense fruitfulness of [your] labours, both the unseen ones and the obvious' (Decree *Perfectae Caritatis* 25). How rich this archdiocese is with religious congregations of both men and women.

Glasgow is home also to new institutes and movements which are a feature of our time, a sign of the seasonal fruitfulness of the Church, which, under the inspiration of the Holy Spirit, provides for each generation's particular needs. My predecessor signally recognised this when he established, as an Archdiocesan Congregation, the Sisters of the Gospel of Life, whose work I will support as best I can.

Those among you who are now retired from the active apostolate must know that the very dedication of your lives is itself an inspiration to us and a reminder of the transcendent values of God's kingdom.

Our faith that the gates of hell will not prevail against the Church is bolstered by our confidence in the prayers of the Virgin Mary, Mother of the Church, under whose mantle I place myself at the beginning of my ministry as your archbishop and to whom I commend this Church of her son our Lord Jesus Christ to whom be glory and honour for ever and ever. Amen.

I pen these final words at the end of a very special day in my life. Last night I took canonical possession of the Archdiocese of Glasgow and was installed as its archbishop. While all this is going on, the College of Consultors of the Diocese of Aberdeen met and elected a new administrator of the diocese, Canon Peter Moran of Inverurie – a member of the Finance Committee and a long-standing friend and colleague. We had gone to Rome together as students in 1952, he from Glasgow and I from Aberdeen, and it is an extraordinary irony that he is now to be Administrator of Aberdeen and I of Glasgow. At twelve noon today we celebrate the installation with mass.

My homilies seem to be well received – certainly yesterday's got positive coverage in this morning's press. Last night there was a reception in the Eyre Hall following the ceremony and today a civic reception is held in the magnificent City Chambers at which I am given a handsome gift of a silver-plate ink stand.

The Lord Provost makes much of the marble work that adorns the interior of the building. Some of it comes from Carrara, not far from my family roots in Italy. I quip in reply that I feel at home already!

FEBRUARY

After the reception we go out for a (very) late lunch to Rogano's and I come back to Newlands Road in a snow storm to find Mrs Mac and Jean, my former housekeeper from Aberdeen, in deepest conversation. (Comparing notes, no doubt, about the archbishop and his culinary perferences!)

I have been overwhelmed by the warmth of the reception I have received from both priests and lay people. Alone now at the end of this day of days, I wonder whether I can live up to their expectations. I realise that I can only do so by being among them, by sharing their joys and sorrows – the words I quoted last night, in fact, from *Gaudium et Spes*, the Second Vatican Council's document on the Church in the Modern World.

This evening, with the festivities over, I read the press and am pleased to find that, generally speaking, it has been generous and kind to me. Long may it last!

I am now ready to go to bed myself.

Lots of love to you all

+Mario

Bishop of Aberdeen

Saturday, 23 February

As I read over last night's diary entry, I realise I must have dropped off several times as I was coming to a close. The result is that the entry ends as though it were a letter and is signed by me, as 'Bishop of Aberdeen' when in fact, there is currently no Bishop of Aberdeen! Nevertheless, I preserve these thoughts as they were written – slips of the pen included!

Monday, 25 February

Mgr Peter Smith has marked this day in my diary for the 'office boys'. It is perhaps an unnecessarily exclusive term since among them is a nun, Sister Veronica, a member of a home-grown order, the Franciscans of the Immaculate Conception. This is, in fact, the only religious order in the Church that has its HQ in Glasgow.

It is good to get together with my closest collaborators now that all the inaugural ceremonies have taken place. It is time to get down to business.

We look at the diary for the next few months, noting commitments which I already have. While I have shed my responsibilities as Bishop of Aberdeen, I have not lost those connected with various national commissions nor, indeed, those responsibilities given to me by the Holy See. Before the end of this week I have two such engagements to fulfil. However, we mark all the free days to be set aside for interviews with the priests of the archdiocese. I will use these interview sessions to get to know the priests, to find out about their parishes and to identify the specific needs or strengths any particular parish might have. It will also be an opportunity for the priests to raise any concerns they may have. In this enterprise, I am greatly supported, not least by the vicar general, Mgr John Gilmartin. He knows the priests of the diocese as well as anyone, having been for many years Director of the Ministry to Priests programme.

Lunch is in the private dining room – an intimate little room with some fine furniture, originally from the archbishop's house, and two paintings on the wall, one of which is, not inappropriately, of cattle. It is good to note that, among all the religious paintings, there are some of secular, even rural scenes!

My predecessor made it his habit to go to the office three times a week – on Mondays, Wednesdays and Fridays. On each day he had pasta with a bolognese sauce, except on Fridays when the sauce had to be prepared without meat. I am amused to recall that that was precisely the pattern of food which he and I enjoyed as students of the Scots College in Rome half a century ago. Indeed, we used to refer to Mondays, Wednesdays and Fridays as 'spag days' and looked forward to them with greater anticipation than the meals on other days – on one of which the experts among us told us that we ate horse. Every description I have ever heard of horse meat would certainly appear to confirm that rumour.

Though I much enjoy my spaghetti, I tell the cook that she can vary her menu and I am amazed in subsequent days what great variety there can be when one has an imaginative *maîtresse de cuisine*.

Tuesday, 26 – Thursday, 28 February

The rest of the week is given to church unity business. At Central Station I meet up with Mgr Henry Docherty, General Secretary of the Bishops' Conference of Scotland, and other delegates to travel with them to Swanwick in Derbyshire for a meeting of what is called the Assembly of CTBI – Churches Together in Britain and Ireland.

There is fun in my reappearing as a long-in-the-tooth ecumenist who has been reinvented as an archbishop. Every opportunity is taken to tease me, particularly when I go missing for one of the sessions I am supposed to be chairing. Gillian Kingston, one of the most able chairpersons and the one who was to introduce me, says simply: 'Lost, one archbishop.' That is, of course, as much title as one will get in such ecumenical gatherings where we are called by our Christian names. I find it somewhat liberating to be just Mario, one of the participants, not necessarily expected to preside or take a leading part.

I recall some years ago at Santiago de Compostella a study group that was ably led by Mrs Nancy Blackie, whose grandparents were, in fact, the builders of the house at Newlands which I now inhabit. She was assisted as Secretary by Bishop Tony Farquhar, Auxiliary Bishop of Down and Connor, and among the participants was the President of the Pontifical Council for the Promotion of Christian Unity, Cardinal Willebrands, who took his turn to make a contribution to the discussion. I even recall what he said. It was a lovely example of ecumenical courtesy, for every time he returned to his native Holland he would go to greet the local pastor in whose parish he would be holidaying. Courtesy, respect for one another – surely an expression of mutual love – is the ground on which the whole ecumenical edifice is constructed. It leads naturally to an exchange of information on all matters of interest to us in our respective churches. It readily prompts co-operation. I have a recollection of another cardinal, the late and much loved Cardinal

Basil Hume, who was in the very hall in which we are meeting today during what was called the 'inter-church process' which led eventually to the formation of CTBI. He said that we must move from co-operation with one another to commitment to one another. It seems to me that we have now reached that stage in which we struggle to give practical expression to our commitment to one another as we journey together towards that goal of organic unity that we recognise as the will of Christ.

At the Last Supper with his disciples, Jesus prayed, '*Ut unum sint*' ('That they all may be one'), giving as model the union which He himself had with his heavenly Father. This is truly an organic union, transcending all manner of associations and federations. The dynamic is the Holy Spirit.

During the course of this week, I have moved from the local (Glasgow) to the national (CTBI) and, tomorrow, it will be to the international scene.

March

Friday, 1 March

I am on my way to Rome to attend an executive meeting of what is called the Joint Working Group (JWG) – a liaison group between the World Council of Churches and the Roman Catholic Church that was set up after the Second Vatican Council. I am privileged to be its Co-Moderator, my colleague being Bishop Jonas Jonson, Lutheran Bishop of Strangnas in Sweden. This meeting is in preparation for the plenary meeting in May, which will take place in Bishop Jonson's own diocese in Sweden.

One of my colleagues on the executive is Sister Elizabeth Moran, a Columban missionary sister. She is well known to me, the sister of Canon Peter Moran who is presently the Administrator of the Diocese of Aberdeen. She worked in the diocese for a number of years, before being seconded, at Rome's request, to work in the area of education and mission – areas in which she is well-qualified, having been a teacher and having worked for some time in the Philippines.

Though the Catholic Church is not a full member of the World Council of Churches, it does work in close partnership with it. We have a new president on the Catholic side of the JWG – a distinguished German theologian, Archbishop Walter Kasper, who was made a cardinal at the last consistory. The bishop-secretary is a French Canadian, Marc Ouillet, soon to be appointed Archbishop of Quebec and primate of Canada.

I recall one parishioner when I was in Caithness. She had once been a telephone operator in quite an important exchange in the north-west of Scotland when they still had to plug lines into different sockets manually. It was possible to overhear conversations and she used to amuse us by telling us of the amount of local gossip that they were able to glean during what might otherwise have been dull moments in working hours. I think of her when I attend these meetings of the executive of the Joint Working Group, because we always dedicate the first session to an exchange of information. The result is that I get a good sense of what is going on in Geneva and in Rome – but none of it is scandalous, I might add!

Monday, 4 March

Today I set off for Aberdeen. I have had time to do little more than change my case since returning from Rome via Birmingham yesterday. I'm going to a meeting of the Scottish Catholic Heritage Commission which had been scheduled before my appointment to Glasgow.

The remit of this commission, of which I am president and which I chair, is to advise bishops on all heritage matters relating to the Catholic Church in Scotland, including the colleges it owns abroad in Rome and Spain. One of its chief interests in recent years has been to consolidate the museum at the former junior seminary at Blairs and to open it to the public on a regular basis. Blairs once contained a very fine library, including books salvaged from the former Scots College in Paris, and the collection was deposited on temporary loan to the National Library of Scotland nearly thirty years ago.

Anticipating the expiry of that loan, the University of Aberdeen has made an approach, through the commission to the bishops as trustees of the Church's heritage, to ask whether it might succeed the National Library as a repository of these books. The Principal of the University, Professor Duncan Rice – himself a graduate of Aberdeen and a man with great ambitions for the university – has conceived of a new humanities resource and research centre. This would be based on a substantial cluster of material encompassing printed, manuscript and microfilm documentation, as well as electronic and digital sources – a library in a new sense and one that would actively recruit students to the study of Scottish history, particularly in the early-modern period. Obviously, the Blairs Library would make a significant contribution to this.

From the beginning the bishops were only minded to agree to the request if it could be shown to improve, in some way, the benefits that scholars already enjoy through the National Library of Scotland. It was because of this additional research element, however, and the knowledge that the Blairs Library would be, in the words of the principal, the 'jewel in the crown' of this new centre that they affirmed their interest in the offer. And so, on this occasion, members of the Heritage Commission have been invited by the principal to visit the present special collections wing of the University Library and to hear from members of staff what was envisaged in the development of the new centre.

It becomes evident to all of us that, if the Blairs Library were to be located in this new centre, then we should actively consider the relocation of the historical section of the Catholic Archives of Scotland – presently sited at Columba House in Edinburgh – as well. Already there has been some concern expressed as to how long the premises at 16 Drummond Place would be sufficient to house the ever-increasing quantity of documentation being sent there from several of the Scottish dioceses and a decision would soon have to be made anyway as to the future location of this archive. This seems an ideal opportunity to expose the historical manuscripts to the study of scholars, whose interest in the printed material would naturally make them gravitate to Aberdeen if the proposal were to succeed.

I am back in my own bed in Aberdeen now. And it would be all too easy to think that what has recently happened was all a dream. But in truth the reality has dawned on me and it is clear that the next few days will be busy, as everyone who has moved house knows only too well. I need to pack cases and trunks and gather my personal papers from the piles on the desk and files in the office.

Saturday, 9 March

I take the 07.21 train to Glasgow in time to attend the formal inauguration of the new centre for The Cardinal Winning Pro-Life

Initiative. In fact, this is the fifth anniversary of the commencement of this scheme, which earned the late Cardinal much praise and not a little criticism – depending on whether you are in favour of helping to take women with crisis pregnancies to full term or prefer to encourage them to seek another solution – in almost every instance, abortion.

Roseann Reddy, whom the Cardinal had placed in charge of this initiative, is already known to me. We have, in the past, shared platforms and, though she did not know it at the time, my sister was really a great admirer of her work, herself being a member of Life – a not dissimilar pro-life body. Roseann had, to much public interest, established herself and two companions as a religious community taking temporary vows of poverty, chastity and obedience under the authority of the Cardinal. They had acquired the tenancy of a house in Holy Cross Parish, right opposite the Church, and their new premises were based in the parish hall a couple of streets away.

I am surprised at the number of people in attendance on this rather cold morning. They are packed into the hall. It is clear many knew one another and they all seem to know Roseann. The late Cardinal's sister, Margaret, is also here, as is his former housekeeper, Mrs Mac, and members of the Cardinal's family. It is right that they should have a role to play in this latest stage of a project in which the Cardinal had invested so much interest and which will, arguably, be one of the most lasting monuments to his pastoral service as Archbishop of Glasgow.

Sunday, 10 March

Twice annually the bishops of Scotland meet for three days, usually at Scotus College in Bearsden, in order to deal with work – both pastoral and administrative – which comes under their joint concern. Cardinal Winning had been President of the Bishops' Conference of Scotland and, following his death, Archbishop Keith O'Brien accepted temporary appointment to this role. The most senior member of the hierarchy – in other words, the archbishop senior by episcopal ordination – is not automatically president, nor is the president the senior member of the hierarchy. Rather, he is its spokesman and chairman, convening meetings of the standing committee and of the Conference itself.

I propose that Archbishop Keith O'Brien, a very good chairman, should be elected president of the Conference and this is unanimously agreed. I am elected vice president. Otherwise, things are as before, including our places round the horseshoe of tables, although Canon Peter Moran joined us to ensure that the Diocese of Aberdeen is represented.

Thursday, 14 March

Today I begin my interviews with the priests of the archdiocese, starting at the end of the alphabet and working towards the beginning. With four a day, on days when I am not otherwise engaged, I work out it will take me well into November – until the Assembly of Priests on 21 November and even beyond – before I will complete this agreeable task.

April

I have been working, during the week, on an article for the *Sunday Herald* on the whole issue of homosexual adoption. Today it is published.

I was recently taken aback by a ruling – outlined in the extract below – from a sheriff whom I knew and for whom I had considerable respect.

In the article I am at pains to avoid polemics, and to make a case based on the distinction between that which is 'right' and those 'rights' that can be given by an institution. My point is that no power on earth can grant a right that is not within their power to give. Unfortunately, the paper – perhaps predictably – has gone for a more lurid headline, which upsets me a bit. The headline is 'Conti: Gays should Not be Parents'. Here is the article.

In a ruling last month, Sheriff Noel McPartlin at Edinburgh Sheriff Court granted 'parental rights and responsibilities' to a lesbian couple. This offers us an opportunity to initiate a debate in Scotland on a range of vitally important issues – all the more topical since, at Glasgow Sheriff Court, around the same time, Sheriff Laura Duncan granted parental rights to the biological father of a child against the wishes of his mother, who is part of a lesbian couple. Duncan, in a robust judgment, stated that a lesbian couple did not constitute 'a family unit', adding that the child's best interests were served though contact with its biological father.

The ruling in the Edinburgh case allows each of the women involved to have parental rights over the other's biological child. The children are the product of a previous marriage and an anonymous sperm donation respectively. The rights were granted in terms of the Children (Scotland) Act 1995, legislation normally used by unmarried fathers, grandparents or step-parents who wish to regularise pre-existing relationships with dependants.

The decision has been described as the granting of 'full parental rights', which raises issues of the origin of such rights. Are they accorded by the state or do they arise naturally from the biological bond between parents and their children and should they, therefore, be protected by law? And what about marriage itself, both as a natural union and a recognised covenant between parents, providing a unique and irreplaceable foundation upon which society is built? A Christian view of society – reflected in the law as we have known it – recognises the natural and inalienable rights of parents over their children.

This would not be to deny that there are circumstances when the welfare of children requires the law to provide alternative arrangements for their upbringing and, therefore, to grant equivalent rights and responsibilities to those who find themselves surrogates. However, the extension of these rights demeans the natural basis of parenthood, a basis that must remain the norm. This is my first concern.

It must always be the welfare of children – not the selfish desires of adults – that is paramount. This leads me into my second area of concern, the definition of welfare. Clearly, in every case, it is necessary to take into account not simply children's material benefits but also their mental, psychological, spiritual and social well-being. With this in mind, it becomes difficult to understand how granting parental rights to same-sex 'parents' can be in the best long-term interests of any child. Leaving aside the moral implications of same-sex relationships, the fact remains that such arrangements are far from society's norm and are likely to remain so.

As such, any child growing up with two 'mothers' or two 'fathers' will unwittingly enter a social and psychological minefield entirely of their guardians' making.

The conflicts, pressures and potential pain of such situations are incalculable. Every adolescent's desire to assimilate with their peers, understand their biological origins and rely on a stable home environment as they make their first forays into adulthood can test even conventional families to the limit; unconventional same-sex 'families' face far greater challenges.

Findings, published earlier this year by the Centre for Policy Studies in a report called 'Broken Hearts', highlight the inherent instability of unmarried parents.

In the document, subtitled 'Family Decline and the Consequences for Society', author, Jill Kirby, presents a range of statistics which are both sobering and deeply worrying. More than half of unmarried co-habiting couples are likely to split within five years of the birth of a child. Of couples who live together and then marry after the birth of a child, a quarter will split within five years compared to only 8 per cent of those married prior to a child's birth.

The instability of homosexual unions is even greater. Long-term stable and single-partner homosexual relationships, although they do exist, are comparatively rare. Almost three-quarters of male homosexuals reported having more than 100 partners during their lifetime, while 28 per cent reported having more than a thousand partners, according to one respected American study.

In Denmark, where a form of homosexual marriage has been legalised since 1989, fewer than 5 per cent of Danish homosexuals have married and over a quarter of these 'marriages' had ended by 1995. Such statistics must give us pause when considering the assessments of children's welfare outside of the marital union.

The case in question is a further step in the disassociating of civil law from its root in natural law. While the love that surrogate parents can give to children in their care has to be recognised and admired, there is no gain for our wider society and certainly not for children themselves in attempts to accord parental rights so widely.

APRIL

Sunday, 21 April

Perhaps predictably, today's *Sunday Herald* carries a number of letters in the wake of last week's article on homosexual adoption which are highly critical of the stance that I took. I can understand that those who are well motivated and are unable to form a natural, heterosexual union feel somewhat aggrieved when what is said implies, to their mind, criticism of their way of life. Of course, the intention of the article was not to be hurtful in any way but to look at the facts behind the stability and longevity of same-sex partnerships, with the inevitable knock-on effect this might have on child welfare, and to explore, in a wider sense, the whole question of rights and defend the unique status of marriage. This was an example to me, I suppose, of the way in which, no matter how carefully in the future I wish to address a subject, I need to be ready for contention and, often enough, misunderstanding of the purpose behind an initiative.

Tuesday, 30 April

I find myself once again on the road north, in my own car but this time not alone. Gerry Beechey, who drives me around as he did my predecessor, is my fellow traveller. He tells me that he has been to Aberdeen before. He drove Cardinal Winning there, when he was still a very young archbishop, for my episcopal ordination twenty-five years ago. The reason for my journey is the silver jubilee of this ordination. Preparations for the celebration have been underway for many months and, indeed, concern as to whether I might be able to mark it in Aberdeen had been my immediate thought on hearing of my appointment to Glasgow.

Twenty-five years ago I had arrived in Aberdeen from a different direction. On that occasion I had travelled from the north and the west – from Caithness to be exact – after nearly fifteen years as a parish priest there. At that time, my biography was almost embarrassingly short! No great list of appointments and offices held. After three years as a curate at St Mary's Cathedral in Aberdeen, I had been appointed as the twenty-eighth parish priest of St Joachim's, Wick, and St Anne's, Thurso, moving to Thurso in 1967. This was the only parish of which I had any experience although it did cover the whole county. My nearest neighbours were, on the landward side, the parish priest of Brora, some fifty miles to the south, and, at an equal distance on the seaward side, the parish priest of Kirkwall in the Orkney Islands. When asked somewhat surprisingly to hear confession on the airport runway, a previous parish priest in the islands is said to have remarked to another priest – apparently off-course like the occasional stray bird: 'You see, to fly south for venial sins is too expensive. To do so for mortal is too dangerous!' An innocent opportunist! Such isolation in his case, as in mine, necessarily made him adjust to his circumstances which resulted in our becoming, when liberated by the Second Vatican Council, ready ecumenists – although I must admit it was a somewhat uphill struggle at times in Wick. Nonetheless, I made good friends there with Church of Scotland, Congregationalist, Episcopal and Salvation Army friends that have stood the test of time.

I came to admire the integrity of those who, while they were not ready for the ecumenical adventure, were nonetheless courteous in their disagreements. My silver jubilee in Aberdeen demonstrates how far we have come ecumenically over the years. My guests include the Episcopal Bishop of Aberdeen and Orkney, the Most Rev. Bruce Cameron, and the Moderator of the Presbytery of Aberdeen, unusually a layman, Dick Wallace. Civic representatives are also prominently present, including the Lord Provost of Aberdeen, Margaret Smith. She is turning the tables on me by hosting a civic dinner in the Beach Ballroom. (When I had become bishop, the dinner for special guests was in an adjacent room and at the expense of the diocese.) It is to be filled, on this occasion, with five hundred guests, invitees of the city. I am greatly honoured by this.

May

Friday, 3 May

The mass in St Mary's Cathedral is splendid. Under George Brand as Master of Ceremonies, the liturgy in the cathedral has always been done beautifully and correctly. A special choir has been formed for this occasion under the direction of a talented musician, David Micheljohn, headmaster of Aboyne Academy, and we have met, on several occasions, to discuss the music. As a result, some of my favourite hymns, such as 'Come Down O Love Divine', which I also had as an entry hymn twenty-five years ago, are included. I certainly did not want *'Ecce Sacerdos Magnus'* ('Behold a Great High Priest (who in his days pleased God)')! A previous Archbishop of Glasgow had objected to the Marian hymn, 'This Is the Image of Our Queen' as he entered his cathedral, as I too had objected in my more modest church in Thurso when I had heard the choir mistress practising 'Little Donkey, Little Donkey On the Way to Bethlehem'. We all have our sensitivities – and you can bet your boots that, even if no member of the laity noticed the hoped-for incongruity, every member of the clergy would!

We also have 'All People That on Earth Do Dwell', another magnificent introit, as well as a most beautiful offertory hymn that was new to me. I wanted children to have a place in the liturgy and a group of pupils from St Joseph's, under a talented senior member of staff, Mrs Patricia Pritchard, mime the offertory theme. I love one of the communion hymns, 'Gifts of Finest Wheat', which had been sung at Bellahouston Park in Glasgow when the pope had celebrated mass there with 300,000 of the faithful in 1982 – a day never to be forgotten. Our giving thanks, our Eucharist, is always celebrated with that finest of God's gifts to us, the Incarnate Son, made present for us in the bread-become-his-body and the wine-become-his-blood. When, at the end of this glorious celebration, the choir sings, as a special tribute:

May the Lord bless you and keep you,
May the Lord let his face shine upon you and be gracious
    unto you,
May the Lord look upon you with kindness and grant you his
    peace.

I struggle to maintain my composure – or, as they might have said in Glasgow, 'I am nearly greetin'.

I had thought hard about my sermon on this occasion. I recalled the words that had touched the late Cardinal Gordon Gray who had ordained me as bishop – a series of references to some of the defining geographical features of the diocese that he had loved. His family hailed from lower Banffshire. I decided to introduce my theme with these same words. I also wanted to include a sentence or two from the sermon that my predecessor in Glasgow, Cardinal Winning, had given at my ordination mass all those years before. In the end I preach the following sermon.

> I am deeply grateful to you all for coming today to share this thanksgiving mass with me on the occasion of the twenty-fifth anniversary of my episcopal ordination in this very cathedral, on the Feast of the Apostles Philip and James.
>
> When the celebration was first mooted, I joked that I might not still be with you, intending my remark as a rather morbid reflection upon the fragility of our hold on life. My remark is now seen, unjustly, as prophetic! However, I am glad that my hold on your affections has outstripped my possession of this chair and that I am still here to address you, albeit it as a former Bishop of Aberdeen and not the subject of a panegyric. Indeed, it is to avoid any semblance of that, that I have chosen to preach myself today!
>
> My way into this homily is provided by St Paul himself in the extract from his First Letter to the Corinthians appointed to be read on this feast: 'Brothers, I want to remind you of the gospel you received and in which you are firmly established' (1 Cor. 15:

MAY

1). And I would like to link this sentence with the first sentence of our first reading from the book of Isaiah: 'How lovely on the mountains are the feet of one who brings good news, who heralds peace, brings happiness, proclaims salvation and tells Zion: "Your God is King!"' (Isaiah 52: 7).

I chose this passage from Isaiah somewhat self-indulgently on account of the nostalgia I feel as I recall my twenty-five years travelling the broad spaces of this lovely diocese. My mosaic of memories is made up of places and of faces. In fact, I could already describe these places in my post-prandial speech of twenty-five years ago, since I came as bishop from within the diocese and after nearly fifteen years as a parish priest in Caithness. I could, therefore, speak of 'the high cliffs of Hoy; the sweeping skyscapes of Caithness; the lonely mountains of Sutherland; the proud peaks of Torridon and Wester Ross; the Grampian Heights and the lovely valleys of the Spey, the Dee and the Don.'

I mentioned some of the places dear to us by reason of the Churches connected with them, places such as 'Eskadale, Fort Augustus, Tynet, Buckie, Pluscarden, Scalan – each telling a story of poverty and patronage, of old places and new fresh hopes.' And the faces? Yes, those dear faces that I recognise here today as representative of many others which flash into my mind as I recall the parishes of the diocese from Lerwick to Stonehaven, from Fraserburgh to Dornie – parishes at the extreme points of the compass which, as I have said more than once, are not peripheral to the diocese but defining markers of its identity.

Of necessity, but not without its pleasure, I fulfilled my mission as bishop of one of the largest and at the same time least populous dioceses in the country as *homo viator*, a 'man on the move'. My life as a bishop has certainly been a physical as well as a spiritual journey. The roads travelled, reflecting these two aspects, can be described equally as the A96 and A9 and as the 'Lord's ways'.

OH HELP!

Bishop Stephen McGill, my revered and ever-popular brother bishop, alone remains of those who assisted at my ordination. He was my Spiritual Director at Blairs and later Rector of the College. On his appointment as Bishop of Argyll and the Isles before his translation to Paisley, he chose, as his episcopal motto, *'Per Tuas Semitas'* – 'Along Your Paths'. Indeed, he and many others during my time as bishop, colleagues both episcopal and priestly, have helped show me the way and have been companions on my journey and I thank them today from the bottom of my heart.

I was nominated bishop by Pope Paul VI on 28 February 1977, twenty-five years, less a week, to the day of my nomination as Archbishop of Glasgow by his successor, Pope John Paul II. It is, perhaps, natural that I should feel indebted to both of them for that favour of the Apostolic See, which, in the time-honoured formula descriptive of a bishop's appointment, is linked with the grace of God. The inspiration of their apostolic ministries has also been a grace.

I should like to share with you some words spoken by Pope Paul VI on his arrival in the Philippines in November 1970 during one of his first and most memorable apostolic journeys. In Manila, before a vast array of the faithful, he presented himself with these words:

> I am sent by Christ, I am an Apostle, I am a Witness. The more distant the goal, the more difficult my mission, the more pressing is the love that urges me to it. I must bear witness to His name: Jesus is the Christ, the Son of the living God, He reveals the invisible God.

On re-reading the sermon given at my ordination by my predecessor in the Archdiocese of Glasgow, Archbishop Thomas Winning, I find that he uses similar words. On that occasion he reminded us: 'The entire life of our Church is centred on him "who is the image of the invisible God, the first born of all creation"' (Col. 1:15). He went on to quote these words from the Second Vatican Council: 'All men are called to union with Christ who is the light of the world, through whom we go forth, through whom we live and towards whom our journey leads us' (*Lumen Gentium* 3).

I return to Pope Paul VI's words: 'He is the companion and friend of our life . . . I could never finish speaking about Him.' He continues with those very words Jesus used of Himself in His conversation with Saint Thomas, as recalled in today's Gospel: 'He is the Way, the Truth and the Life.' And then he adds: 'He is the King of the new world; He is the secret of history; He is the key to our destiny; He is the mediator, the bridge between heaven and earth.'

'The Way . . . the bridge between heaven and earth.' This coincidence of imagery of the road and of the bridge, describing as it does the more theological term, 'mediator', leads us, I believe, to see Christ not only in terms of his divine personhood but also in the more concrete reality of his humanity. Ever greater is the need to present Christ to the men and women of our age, not only in the essential but more remote terms of his divinity but in that shared humanity which he assumed in order to transform it.

The human personality of Christ shines out from the Gospel pages. The love of Pope Paul VI was for a man whose compassion and love met the needs of all mankind. He could quote the words of the Second Vatican Council that Jesus Christ, true God and true Man, loves the world 'with a human heart' (*Gaudium et Spes* 22).

'Wisest love,' in Cardinal Newman's memorable words, 'that flesh and blood which did in Adam fail should strive afresh against the foe, should strive and should prevail!'

The great Spanish mystic, Saint Teresa of Avila, capable of the most sublime ecstasies of union with God, was once advised by a spiritual director to forget the humanity of Christ and focus instead on His divinity. She subsequently reported, with typical forthrightness, that, having tried to do this for several weeks, she recognised her mistake. It is only in grasping the humanity of Christ that we poor human beings can come to know and embrace the invisible God.

'To have seen me is to have seen the Father,' said Jesus to Philip, 'so how can you say, "Let us see the Father?" Do you not believe that I am in the Father and the Father is in me?' (John 14: 9). The comforting corollary of this emphasis on the humanity of Christ is that we who are ordained to act *'in persona Christi'* – 'in Christ's name and person' – are able to bring to the task our own fragile humanity and place it at the service of Christ.

Pope John Paul II, as a young bishop at the Vatican Council, was moved, when attending an ordination in St Peter's, and wrote a poem in recollection of the prostrated body of the priest:

> You are the floor that others may walk over you . . .
> Not knowing where they go you guide their steps . . .
> You want to serve their feet that pass,
> As rocks serve the hooves of sheep.
>
> ('The Church, Shepherds and Springs', 1962)

Dear friends, let me hasten to assure you that my use of this quotation is not an oblique complaint that, during my time as your bishop, you have trampled on me! On the contrary, I have been sustained by your friendship. The point I really want to make is that human friendship is one of the most precious treasures we have and it is the ground of our communion, not only with one another but with God Himself, in the great redeemed humanity of the Church: 'This is my body; this is my blood'.

I sense that, in the prevalent culture of today, humanity as a virtue is not highly regarded, nor is humanity, in the sense of that commonality of being that is natural to us, truly appreciated for what it is; something given – a gift we receive and not something we construct. Our human friendships, human relationships and that very special interpersonal union which we refer to as conjugal love and of which the human family is itself the gift – all of these are traduced and demeaned if they are understood as mere constructs. For, if they are constructs, they are, therefore, capable of deconstruction or of the insult of equating them with what is, so often, a sad parody of what it is to be truly human, male and female, 'made in the image and likeness of God' (Gen. 1: 27).

However, it soon becomes very clear to us that we need a key to unlock the meaning of 'true humanity'. 'He is the key . . .' said Pope Paul VI referring to Christ. In truth, He is our exemplar or model against whom our humanity is to be measured, our human relationships calibrated and, as the Apostle said, on whom 'every structure is aligned'. 'You too, in Him, are being built into a house where God lives in the Spirit' (Eph. 2: 22).

If I have succeeded at all where I tried to align this Holy Church of Aberdeen on Him, during the twenty-five years of my ministry among you, and done so conscious that there are other stones who belong also to this building, I may be allowed to express the hope of the same Apostle who said to the Corinthians: 'By the grace God gave me, I succeeded as an architect and laid the foundations, on which someone else is doing the building.' And may I continue to borrow his words? 'Everyone doing the building must work carefully . . . For the foundation, nobody can lay any other than the one which has already been laid, that is Jesus Christ' (1 Cor. 3: 9–11).

May His love sustain us and may she, from whom he took humanity and who now shares His glory, be our constant intercessor at the throne of grace.

The mass is concelebrated by a cohort of bishops and priests, my colleagues in the Scottish hierarchy doing me the honour of attending along with bishop friends from Regensburg (Aberdeen's twin city), Trondheim (Aberdeen's neighbour across the North Sea) and from Belfast and Limerick (beyond the Irish Sea). Archbishop Vincent Nichols of Birmingham, who had missed my installation in Glasgow due to a hip operation, is happily present, as is the apostolic nuncio, who delivers a most moving letter from the Holy Father. It is customary for the pope to mark the jubilees of bishops in this way. I could not think of a message that would have meant more to me than his – unless one from my mother beyond the heavens!

'Wouldn't she have been proud,' said my cousin Hilda, present with her daughters, Carole and Heather, alongside my brother-in-law, Noel, and my nieces and nephews, Margaret (with Paul and my great-nieces Josephine and Michelle), Jacinta (with Liam and their infant in the womb), Damian (with Jane and their three children, Jacob, Woody and Zoe) and John (with his girlfriend Melanie). My cousin Bobby, from Lossiemouth, is there too (with Cathy) and my sister Stella's friends have come from Birmingham, in a sense representing her since she is still unable to travel.

The words of the Holy Father's letter virtually conclude the mass, at the end of which, to the sound of a hundred bell changes, the guests leave by bus for a reception and lunch at the Altens Thistle Hotel. My family and special guests are accommodated there for the few days of the celebrations. The pope's words are still beguiling my ears as I am carried by donated limousine to the hotel.

Canon Peter Moran, the Diocesan Administrator, speaks for the diocese at the buffet reception and gives me, on behalf of the Chapter of Canons, a set of breviaries – the three books which contain the daily readings, psalms and prayers which every priest and bishop is required to use. Many others, including deacons and members of religious orders, use these prayers in part. Priests wedded to these books have, in the past, sometimes referred to them as 'the Missus'. If every set were a wife, I would now be in charge of a harem, given the number I have and have inherited! As a token and token message, the gift is nonetheless very acceptable.

MAY

Saturday, 4 May

The civic lunch is a splendid affair with the Lord Provost wearing her gold chain of office and being flanked at the top table by special guests, including Archbishop Keith O'Brien of St Andrews and Edinburgh, Bishop George Müller of Trondheim and Bishop Manfred Müller of Regensburg.

The cathedral in Regensburgh, a slightly smaller version of Cologne's great pile, has several choirs, perhaps the most famous of which is the Domspazen – literally the 'cathedral sparrows' and composed, you've guessed it, of boys and very young men. With a tradition spanning back a thousand years(!), they have a reputation similar to the perhaps better-known Vienna Boys' Choir. My gift from Regensburg – and from Aberdeen, which sponsored their coming – is their participation first of all at the civic lunch (by 'singing for their supper') and, secondly, at a concert in the Chapel of Blairs College in the evening, which proves to be delightful beyond description.

The Lord Provost is gracious in her address, at the end of which she gives me a parchment scroll on which my good behaviour is recorded – I felt like a schoolboy at prize-giving but none is ever prouder – and two tapestry cushions decorated with the arms of the city: its shield of three towers supported by leopards.

I reply to the toast by recalling the historic connection between the bishopric and the city, both granted royal charters in the 1130s by King David I, the saintly son of Queen Margaret. The episcopal burgh still goes under its original name Aberdon, in the *Annuario Pontificio*, the Directory of the Holy See. Its location at the mouth of the Don is matched by the royal burgh's position at the mouth of the Dee. Aberdeen now embraces them both.

Sunday, 5 May

I celebrate mass at 11.15 a.m. in St Mary's Cathedral. The Ceremonial of Bishops recommends that a bishop at the end of his pastorate should be suitably bidden farewell in his cathedral church. The clerestory windows of the lofty building admit the midday sun, gilding the tall sandstone columns of the nave and falling as a pool of light on the steps of the cathedra. As a metaphor of beauty, it describes the sound of the boys' choir, soaring upwards into the rafted space of the high nave. Once again the building trembles to the sound of Ronald Leith at the great organ. Such are the memories, more tangible than the written word, that I enfold – the context of many personal words of farewell from a lovely people.

I have always been proud to have been associated with this dour and dignified city – the silver city by the silver sea – so vibrant now, not only as a place of learning and commerce, of fish and agricultural markets, of banks and law offices, but as the nerve-centre of the North Sea oil industry. It is true that the Church and the churches no longer hold a balance of power or influence in the community and are certainly not great contributors, as in the past, to its wealth. However, I believe their benign influence in the form of education and pastoral care continues to benefit the citizens of the city and the inhabitants of a much wider area.

After the civic lunch, one of my sister's friends from Solihull remarks that he feels proud to be a Catholic in Aberdeen. It sums up the feeling of the entire Catholic community in face of the generous recognition accorded me by the city.

Meanwhile, the Regensburgh choirboys had been accommodated in family homes in the city – some of which had to be persuaded to give up their charming charges when the weekend was over. So Joyce Webster, the Diocesan Administration Officer, told me – she who had magnificently masterminded the whole affair.

Wednesday, 8 May

There's a request today from *The Scotsman*, asking me about my favourite restaurant. They are doing a series on the culinary preferences of the 'great and good', among whom I am apparently now numbered! The answer was easy to give.

I recall with great fondness Kinloch Lodge on the Isle of Skye. It is an ancestral home of the Macdonald clan and is awash in history and culture. From the windows one can admire the Cuillin Hills or, with luck, the sweep of a golden eagle or an otter playing in Loch na Dal. It's here, in this quite magnificent setting, that Lady Claire and Lord Godfrey Macdonald prepare some of the finest food in the land.

Some years ago I came to Skye to confer the sacrament of confirmation on Lord Godfrey, a convert to the Catholic faith. There was no Catholic church there at the time and I remember the confirmation ceremony took place in a doctor's surgery! Afterwards we retired to Kinloch Lodge for a meal – and what a meal it was. The starter was a hot-smoked salmon terrine, followed by roast rack of Highland-bred lamb. As I was enjoying the superb food, it occurred to me that I seemed to recognise Lord Godfrey's godmother, though I couldn't quite place her. Gradually it dawned on me. The lady in question was none other than Clarissa Dickson Wright.

The food was memorable, the company was wonderful, the setting was magnificent. Need I say more.

Wednesday, 15 May

What unusual requests arrive at this office! Today's comes from the National Libraries of Scotland, who are preparing an exhibition on childhood reading habits. I'm being asked to name a book that influenced me as a child and this will then be included in an exhibition in Edinburgh later in the year.

I recall with great fondness reading a series of books by Joan Windham called *The Six O'Clock Saints*. They were very accessible little works, each well illustrated and containing some of the more memorable lives of the saints. The following is from the entry on St Frances of Rome:

> That you can be a saint,
> In quite a rich home,
> Is shown by the case
> Of Saint Frances of Rome.

She had plenty of children,
A husband, a cook,
A household to manage,
A housekeeping book –
And they kept her so busy
Both up and downstairs
She couldn't think when
To get on with her prayers.
She no sooner was kneeling
Than someone would call –
She thought she would never
Get finished at all.
First her husband must see her,
Then up came the cook,
Then a little boy shouting
To please come and look –
Then a friend with a very
Long story to tell,
And a dozen poor people
With troubles as well.
And she never lost patience,
Or said, 'Not at home,'
And that's why we call her
Saint Frances of Rome.

Looking back, the tone is of another age – the 1930s and '40s – and the poetry wouldn't win any prizes today. Nevertheless, I did become fascinated in later life to read more about the lives of those saints that I had become acquainted with in this series.

Wednesday, 22 May

A request from *The Journalist's Handbook* arrives today asking me to write something about my choice of adult reading.

Since I moved to Glasgow to take up my new duties here, I have changed my reading habits. After a lifetime of the *Press and Journal*,

MAY

I have now switched to *The Herald* and *Sunday Herald*, accompanied by *The Scotsman* and *Scotland on Sunday*.

Every week I also look forward to reading through *The Tablet*. Though I may not always agree with its contents, it remains a stimulating read for all who have an interest in religion and public affairs.

Another regular is the *Osservatore Romano*, the newspaper of the Holy See, which has a weekly English language edition. It is a very useful compendium of the output of the various departments of the Roman Curia, as well as the statements and sermons of the pope.

A number of reviews and periodicals also come 'with the job', one of the more prestigious of which is the *Civilta' Cattolica*. This is the Jesuit-run review of society, ethics and politics that is published in Italian every fortnight and whose editorials are often a good barometer of opinion at the highest echelons of the Church.

Away from 'professional' reading, I enjoy *National Geographic*. I came across the magazine rather by accident, since I inherited a subscription from my predecessor as Bishop of Aberdeen all those years ago. It is a fascinating read, outstanding in its scope and anthropological content, and I enjoyed the copies I received so much that I've continued the subscription ever since.

Rather less well-known is the *Giornale di Barga*, the newspaper produced in the area of Tuscany from which my grandparents emigrated to Britain a century ago. It is full of interesting information, even to second-generation expats like myself, and has even been known to carry the occasional article about a certain 'Toscano' who is currently Archbishop of Glasgow!

Thursday, 23 May

This afternoon, at 2.30 p.m. precisely and with the sort of precision that accompanies all such events, the Queen and Prince Philip are met at the great west door of St Mungo's Cathedral for the national service of thanksgiving to mark her golden jubilee as Queen. I am one of those seated in the sanctuary area awaiting their arrival.

Beside and in front of me are other Church leaders and all around are the representatives of other faiths, of the Scottish Parliament, of the law and other great institutions of state. The Lord Provosts are wearing their heavy gold chains of office and soldiers their medals. I am dressed in the distinctive choir-dress of a Catholic bishop – magenta in colour with a plain gold cross that I had chosen from the archdiocesan treasury in preference to the many chaste and jewelled versions used by my predecessors. I don't know how often, if at all, my post-Reformation predecessors had been 'robed and in the sanctuary' in what was once the seat of the Archbishops of Glasgow. But I have to admit I am very proud to be there and taking part in a glorious event for a queen who holds her crown in direct descent from Mary, Queen of Scots, and King James VI and I – whom my last medieval predecessor, Archbishop Beaton, served as ambassador in Paris where he died in the very year of the union of the crowns, 1603.

The Moderator of the General Assembly of the Church of Scotland, the Rt Rev. John Miller, himself a minister of a Glasgow parish, gives the sermon in which he strikes all the right notes as do, in a literal sense, the excellent choir.

At the end we form a great procession leading the Queen, Prince Philip and their entourage to the door. Most of us are shunted into a siding while the minister of the cathedral, Dr William Morris, and the Moderator bid Her Majesty goodbye.

Friday, 24 May – Friday, 31 May
I have heard that there is to be a garden party at Holyrood Palace on the day following the service at Glasgow Cathedral. So, in order to make myself available, I have arranged to leave from Edinburgh Airport instead of Glasgow for my first ever visit to Sweden to attend the plenary meeting of the Joint Working Group. In the end, the invitation does not come, which just shows that you must never take these things for granted! And so, a day late and from Edinburgh, I travel to London and then onwards, after a night's stop-over in a hotel in Stansted, on a cheap flight to Sweden.

Thirty-one members attend the plenary, representing the Catholic Church and the World Council of Churches. We are accommodated in a beautifully situated retreat house at Stjarnholm in Strangnas, the diocese of Bishop Jonas Jonson who is the Joint Working Group's Co-Moderator. Travelling by bus to the centre, I am struck by the gentle pastoral character of the landscape, with fields alternating with deep forests.

Horses were being exercised in front of the house, which had at one time been the home of a well-to-do Swedish family. It is beautifully appointed, with a lovely light and airy chapel at which we have our daily services.

On Sunday, 26 May we go to the Cathedral of Strangnas for a celebration of baptism, confirmation and High Mass according to the tradition of the Church of Sweden. Bishop Jonson presides over the liturgy and I give the homily. I am told it is the first time since the Reformation that a Catholic bishop, let alone an archbishop, has preached here.

It is an extremely commodious and handsome building, dating from the late medieval period and constructed of brick, a building material to which we are unaccustomed for cathedrals in Britain. There are exceptions, of course – St Alban's, where part of the cathedral is built of brick taken from the old Roman city and, of course, the more recent splendid example of Westminster Cathedral in London. Another unaccustomed feature of a Swedish medieval church is that the medieval ornaments – the statues and wall-paintings – have survived, Sweden not knowing the iconoclastic actions of the English and Scottish reformers. The Lutheran worship is also much closer to what Catholics are used to. I will always remember the baptism of a couple of teenagers who were supported by their peers, who then went with them to kneel round the altar to be confirmed by the laying-on of hands of the Lutheran bishop. In Catholic and Orthodox confirmations, the laying-on of hands is accompanied by anointing with the oil of chrism, an oil which is perfumed with balsam or some other scent.

It is Trinity Sunday in the Christian calendar and one of the readings is taken from St Paul's Second Letter to the Corinthians: 'Greet one another with a holy kiss. All the saints send you greetings . . . the grace of the Lord Jesus Christ, the love of God and the fellowship of the Holy Spirit be with you all' (2 Cor. 13: 11–13). I continue:

> These are appropriate words in the mouth of one invited to address you, one who comes to you from a country across the North Sea and from another Church – an archbishop who is a colleague of your own bishop in the Joint Working Group and who shares with him the Apostolic faith in the Divinity of Christ, the Fatherhood of God and the Divine Mission of the Holy Spirit. We celebrate, on this Sunday after Pentecost, the feast of the Holy Trinity.
>
> St Columbanus, one of the greatest Celtic missionaries, who gave back to Europe what he himself had received from the Heralds of the Gospel, asks rhetorically:

> Who then is God? He is Father, Son and Holy Spirit, one God. Seek no further concerning God; for those who wish to know the great deep must first review the natural world. For knowledge of the Trinity is properly likened to the depths of the sea, according to that saying of the Sage, 'And the great deep, who shall fathom it?' Since just as the depth of the sea is invisible to human sight, even so the Godhead of the Trinity is found to be unknowable by human senses. And, thus, if I say a man wishes to know what he ought to believe, let him not think that he understands better by speech than by believing; because when he seeks it, knowledge of the Godhead will recede further than it was. (St Columbanus, *Instruction on Faith*, 3–5)

> These are magnificent words, instilling in us a sense of awe before the great mystery we celebrate.
>
> With Moses, we feel we should bow down to the ground and

worship (Exod. 34: 8). But can we not seek knowledge of God without the Godhead receding further from us? The scholastics attempted the quest through the *'via negativa'*, as it was called – by systematically declaring what God was not and so removing from us any sense that God is like us in our contingent existence, our temporal limitations, our geographical containment, our impotence to do anything other than what is allowed us. They emphasised the transcendence of God.

But God is also immanent. 'God is everywhere,' says St Columbanus. 'Utterly vast, and (paradoxically) everywhere near at hand. "For in Him", as the Apostle says, "we live and move and have our being"' (Acts 17: 28).

The solution Columbanus offers our otherwise impotent quest is the way of faith:

> Seek the supreme wisdom, not by verbal debate, but by the perfection of a good life, not with the tongue, but with the faith which issues from singleness of heart, not that which is gathered from the guests of a learned irreligion . . .

And he promises comfortingly, 'Wisdom shall stand at her accustomed station at the gate' (St Columbanus, *Instruction on Faith*: 3–5).

Who is this gatekeeper if not Christ, through whom we enter the sheepfold – and the mystery of God? 'Jesus said to Nicodemus: God loved the world so much that He gave His Son so that anyone who believes in Him may have eternal life' (John 3: 16). And in another place we read: 'Eternal life is this: to know the only true God and Jesus Christ whom He has sent' (ibid. 17: 3).

Most certainly Christ is the key and our faith in Him as Son of God, is the opening to an appreciation – some attainment – of the mystery of the Holy Trinity in a manner, in Columbanus' words but redolent of St Paul, 'that passes understanding . . . partly seen by the pure heart' (ibid.).

I am struck by the thought that, when faced with another mystery, our surest path to its attainment may well be the same as that by which, in some measure, we attain the mystery of the Godhead. The mystery of which I speak is related to that of the Holy Trinity.

Jesus said, 'Holy Father, keep those You have given Me true to Your name, so that they may be one in Us, as You are in Me and I am in You' (John 17: 11). This unity which we seek is not simply that of friendship, though it presumes it; not that of common social action or service, though it will foster it; nor even that of a federation or community of willing parties, though this may in part result from it. Rather, the unity we seek is a dynamic force which animates us from within. It is a unity which is not obtained by 'verbal debate, but by the perfection of a good life, not with the tongue, but with the faith which issues from singleness of heart, not with that which is gathered from the guests of a learned irreligion'. And we are assured again that 'Wisdom shall stand at her accustomed station at the gate' (St Columbanus, op. cit. 3–5).

The dynamic of which we speak is described in this context by the Greek word '*koinonia*', in Latin, '*communio*'. Cardinal Walter Kasper, President of the Pontifical Council for the Promotion of Christian Unity, recently noted with some astonishment that, though the many dialogues in which the Catholic Church is a partner 'were never held according to a pre-conceived idea', nevertheless, all of them, 'both with the Orthodox Churches and with the Anglican Communion, with the Lutheran and Reformed ecclesial communities, the Free Churches and the new Evangelical and Pentecostal communities – all converge in the fact that they centre around the concept of communio' (Discourse at Plenary of Pontifical Council, 2001).

Communio really is the key concept for all bilateral and multilateral dialogues. And in each of these dialogues *communio* can be understood in analogy with the original Trinitarian model, not as uniformity, but as unity in diversity and diversity in unity.

This understanding helps clarify some thoughts which have perhaps not been well understood in the years following Vatican

104

II [the Second Vatican Council]. If, according to the Council's teaching, the unity of the Church of Jesus Christ is realised already – 'subsists' – in the Catholic Church (*Lumen Gentium* 8), we are not to read this in an exclusive way. It implies that the many elements of ecclesial reality are already present in other churches and ecclesial communities.

In baptism, we have the sacramental basis for *communio*. In recognising one another's baptism as being the one baptism of which St Paul speaks – 'one faith, one baptism' (Eph. 4: 15) – we acknowledge an existing unity or communio; imperfect but real.

In the Eucharist, we look forward to the sacramental completion of perfect unity. In all the sacraments, we have the effective sign of that Spirit whose gift and operation is the dynamic which in all our dialogues but, above all, in the dialogue of prayer, we seek . . . with a humble heart.

I give this homily in English and am surprised at how the congregation appears to be following me, although they had been give a translation in Swedish prepared by Bishop Jonas himself. There is one little misunderstanding when he translates 'Columbanus' as 'Columba', assuming that I am referring to our Scottish missionary. I am, however, referring to the Irish monk who, in the great tradition of those Irish missionaries, travelled deep into Europe and founded the famous monastery of Bobbio, in Liguria, which became an important centre of learning and missionary activity in the north of Italy.

We process out of the cathedral into the sunlit forecourt, where we are warmly greeted by the large congregation that has attended the service. Thereafter, we walk downhill to the bishop's palace and are entertained to lunch by Bishop Jonas and his wife, Brigitta Rubenson.

On we travel to Stockholm, well deserving its reputation as one of the loveliest European capitals. It is built round a great harbour, which we explore on a boat before gathering at the modern Catholic Cathedral for mass and a reception. We meet the Catholic bishop,

Bishop Anders Arborelius, with his auxiliary bishop, an Englishman named William Kenny, and other Church leaders during the course of the week.

It is not all play, of course. Our agenda includes such heavyweight subjects as 'The Ecclesiological Consequences of Baptism'; 'Inter-Church Marriages'; 'Theological Anthropology'; 'National and Regional Councils of Churches'; and 'The Nature and Purpose of Ecumenical Dialogue'. Bishop Jonas and I take it in turns to moderate the sessions, each of us, I suspect, trying to avoid being responsible for the section on theological anthropology!

June

These ten days see me, if not like the proverbial headless chicken, nonetheless flapping about from north to south and back again, largely because of the Queen's jubilee.

On Sunday at 3 p.m., I celebrate a mass of thanksgiving in St Andrew's Cathedral. On the Monday, I am off to London where I stay with my friend, Cardinal Cormac Murphy O'Connor. On Tuesday, I go with him to St Paul's Cathedral for the magnificent national celebration of the Queen's Golden Jubilee.

Security is tight and many of the streets in central London are cordoned off, although there are masses of good-natured people with whom the London bobbies are bantering in typical fashion. Somewhere around Whitehall the Cardinal's driver manages to break through the cordon and, once we are in, it seems that nothing can stop us from proceeding along the royal route to St Paul's itself.

The people waiting expectantly for something to happen are delighted at this interlude but I have to admit that I slip further and further down the back seat out of embarrassment. I sense what it must be like being royalty, with people peering at you from all sides – in this instance, of course, wondering who on earth it is in the back of the car. The Cardinal in the front seat, tall man that he is, has no chance of slipping down even if he wanted to. On the contrary, he seems very content to be seen and has stuck a notice on the front window of the car saying 'The Cardinal Archbishop of Westminster'. I think that this might be to ensure we would not be shot at – or, rather, since the mood is anything but belligerent, that we will progress unhindered. And this is precisely what we do up the hill to St Paul's, where the bells are ringing and all is festive. Then we have a magnificent sermon and are captivated by the wonderful singing of a work by John Rutter that beguiles us all with its beauty as boys' voices echo round the drum of the great dome. I return to Glasgow that night.

On Wednesday, I go to a cocktail party at Boturich Castle given by the Lord Lieutenant of Dunbartonshire. The setting, overlooking Loch Lomond, is splendid; the food and entertainment are wonderful; the midgies are appalling! I thought it was only in the north-west Highlands that they were so well dragooned.

On Friday, I am off to Thurso, there to celebrate, in what for nearly fifteen years had been my one and only parish when parish priest, my silver jubilee as a bishop – truly from one end of the country to another. As I predicted, among the events is a delightful concert given by the Thurso Musical Ensemble in St Anne's Church.

On Monday, I am back in London again – this time for a reception at Buckingham Palace. When first I was told of this invitation, the Chancellor had said that the Queen had invited me along with some other church leaders to meet her. Subsequently, I was told that the gathering would be in the White Drawing-Room and that I should present myself at the palace at an agreed time. My vision was of a douce tête-à-tête over tea with Her Majesty.

I had become aware that Cardinal Murphy O'Connor was going to be there as well and, of course, I didn't mind sharing the event with him. Indeed, it was greatly to my advantage since his enterprising driver was once more called upon to get us to the palace on time. No solitary journey this time. We struggle with taxis galore that we eventually realise were all making in the same general direction – yes, to Buckingham Palace.

I am, indeed, introduced to Her Majesty in the White Drawing-Room along with a select number of Church and other faith leaders as we stand in a large circle. Following Her Majesty is the Duke of Edinburgh, the Prince of Wales and countless other members of the royal family who subsequently take up assigned positions in adjacent drawing-rooms where 600 others – Church leaders, that is – have gathered!

The Catholic bishops, even Cardinals, are sartorially outshone on this occasion. I am soberly dressed in a black suit with a silver pectoral cross round my neck. 'It's not real silver!' the pope's secretary had whispered to me when the Holy Father had handed it over on the occasion of a previous trip to Rome.

Prince Philip says to me, 'That's not how you were dressed the other day,' referring to Glasgow Cathedral.

'No,' I say, 'I left my glad rags behind!'

'You are dressed for a funeral!' he says jokingly before moving on.

A day for someone else to shine, I think!

Sunday, 23 June

Today I have my first ordination of a new priest as Archbishop of Glasgow. He is Dr Frank Wilson, well known in Glasgow medical circles. After years of caring for men's bodies (and women's too for that matter!), he is now to serve their souls.

The mass takes place at the magnificent church of Christ the King in King's Park and a great turnout of the clergy is duly marshalled. From the corner of my eye I notice a few of the older priests stumble at the end of the long procession. At that precise moment they need a doctor more than a priest but, since the church is half-full of medics (Frank's former colleagues), there can be no better time to faint!

There are no complications, I am glad to report. But there are two latecomers, one of whom appears to be dressing still, much to the displeasure of the master of ceremonies, my Chancellor, who makes a beeline for them that seems to go straight through me – much to my momentary alarm! Otherwise, all was decorous and dutiful. The lines of the psalmist come to mind: '*Bonum et iucundum fratres in unum*' – 'How good and happy it is to be brothers together.'

I go straight from the church to Glasgow Airport to take a plane to Gatwick for tomorrow's assembly of the Order of Malta and the celebration of the their patronal feast of St John the Baptist.

Originally a group of hospitaller monks in Jerusalem, it grew into a knightly order when it became necessary to have men of arms to defend the pilgrims on their way to Jerusalem. They became a power in the land but were eventually driven out of Palestine and then Rhodes, where, to this day, remnants of the great hospital they built there can still be seen.

It was Suliman the Magnificent who drove them out of Rhodes. In view of their valour, they were allowed to retreat with military honours. Eventually they found a home in Malta, given to them as a fief by the Emperor Charles V. They then withstood a great siege and built the fortified harbour and city of Valletta, named after their grand master, de Vallette. In the great hospital there, they served the sick, their 'lords', on silver plates and in fine beds, a level of service to be repeated but never surpassed. They built and maintained a great fleet of galleons as well, with which they defended the soft underbelly of Christian Europe against the incursions of the Muslim Turks.

Again expelled, this time by Napoleon – ironically, a Christian Emperor – they were welcomed to Rome from where they still administer their order from a fine palace on the fashionable Via Condotti. Over their palace flies their flag, as proudly as the Royal Standard does over Buckingham Palace, indicating the presence of their prince and grand master. He is currently Frà Andrew Bertie, an Englishman with Scottish connections, his mother being a member of the Crichton-Stuart family, the Marquesses of Bute.

I have been a chaplain to the British Association of the Knights of Malta for many years. For five years I was their principal chaplain, celebrating mass, attending their Lourdes pilgrimages and generally supporting their charitable work through which they continue their traditional care of the sick.

Thursday, 27 June

Today I leave Gatwick for Rome where I am met by the vice rector of the Scots College, Fr Paul Milarvie. As a metropolitan archbishop, I am required to seek from the pope the pallium, a symbol of metropolitan authority.

During most of the medieval period – before the Reformation –

Glasgow was a bishopric subject to the Papacy since it resisted the claims of York to metropolitan oversight. Indeed, in 1175 Pope Alexander III had addressed Glasgow as *'Specialis Filia Romanae Ecclesiae'* ('Special Daughter of the Roman Church').

In 1492 the city acquired metropolitan status in rivalry to St Andrews. After the Reformation, in 1603, and following the death of Archbishop Beaton, Glasgow was effectively defunct as a Catholic archbishopric. It remained vacant for almost three centuries.

At the restoration of the heirarchy in 1878, Glasgow was left in an equally anomalous situation – it was made an archbishopric without a metropolitan province, just as it had once been a bishopric without an overseeing Metropolitan See. All of this was remedied in 1947 when the bishoprics of Paisley and Motherwell were carved out of the territory of the Archdiocese of Glasgow by Pope Pius XII to form a new province.

Much was made, in 1922 – the 500th anniversary of the archbishopric – of its special relationship with the Holy See. The truth is, however, that so complete was the success of the Presbyterian reform of the Scottish Church that, by the late eighteenth century, there was no more than a dozen known Catholics in the city. But the Industrial Revolution, which was to change the fortunes of the city, was also to alter its denominational face. The strong Catholic presence today in Glasgow and the industrial West of Scotland owes its origins to the arrival of Catholic Highlanders and Irish immigrants. The fidelity to the Catholic Church and the Holy See of both these groups, in the face of persecution and grinding poverty, justifies Glasgow Archdiocese's present proud adherence to its status as 'Special Daughter'.

Tonight I am a guest of honour at a dinner given by the British Ambassador to the Holy See at the very beautiful embassy by the Porta Latina – its garden stretching towards and contained within the old Roman walls.

I am delighted that so many of my Roman friends are present, including a companion from Blairs days, Mgr Charlie Burns OBE,

111

lately retired from work at the Secret Archives of the Vatican.

I now have a couple of days to relax – the first since my installation. Walking up and down in the warm Roman sunshine on the terrazza of the Scots College, I recall not only my past days in Rome but also Rome's past days. I have an acute attack of nostalgia, prompted perhaps by the fact that, a few days ago, I was staying at the London Oratory, the fathers of which are the spiritual heirs of St Philip Neri, called the Second Apostle of Rome. My grandfather's name was Philip – Filippo Aemiliano Panicali. He came, as did my paternal grandfather, Joseph Conti, from St Philip Neri's land of Tuscany. In fact, the saint was a Florentine who made his home in Rome. And, during the compulsory spiritual reading exercises that preceded lunch in my student days at the Scots College, I read page by page Fr John Broderick's comprehensive life of the saint.

Rome is layered. Whether your interest is in the classical period or the medieval, the early renaissance or the baroque, you can fill your soul with what this city has to offer. I certainly have a love for the antique, whether pagan or Christian, but my favourite Rome is the Rome of St Philip Neri's time.

It is the Rome of the late Renaissance, of the first stirrings of the Reform (the counter-Reformation); the Rome of the Council – albeit that the Council was held in the foothills of the Alps; the Rome of a new spring, whose art and architecture, literature and music, while it continued its rapid flowering, became more and more expressive of the Christian, the Catholic, spirit to whose service it was now rededicated.

It is the Rome of Sixtus V, of St Pius V, of the short-lived Marcellus II, in whose memory Palestrina wrote the 'Missa Papae Marcelli' (the 'Mass of Pope Marcellus'), of Paul IV, of Gregory XIV and Clement VIII. Clement was the founder of the Scots College and a confidant of Philip, who had chided his friend the pope about the infrequency of his visits. Clement replied, 'And when next our Lord comes to see you, pray for me and the pressing needs of Christendom.' The correspondence of popes is now with saints

Making an entrance. My arrival at the door of St Andrew's Cathedral to be installed as Archbishop, 21 February 2002.

Kissing the cross held by Mgr Martin Quinlan at the door of the Cathedral, 21 February 2002.

Fancy meeting you here! Cousin Agostino Caproni (left) and Mgr Piero Giannini (right) who travelled from Barga for the ceremonies, 22 February 2002.

A lonely moment: kneeling in prayer before taking possession of the Cathedral, 21 February 2002.

All the best! First Minister Jack McConnell offers his congratulations, 21 February 2002.

Meet the family (left to right): With Luana McKenna, Agostino Caproni and Clara Piacentini, 22 February 2002.

Meeting the locals on my first parish visit as Archbishop, St John Ogilvie's Easterhouse, 10 March 2002.

First meeting with Prime Minister Tony Blair and wife Cherie at the opening of St Andrew's Secondary, 20 June 2002.

The laying on of hands: a moment from the ordination of Fr Frank Wilson, 23 June 2002.

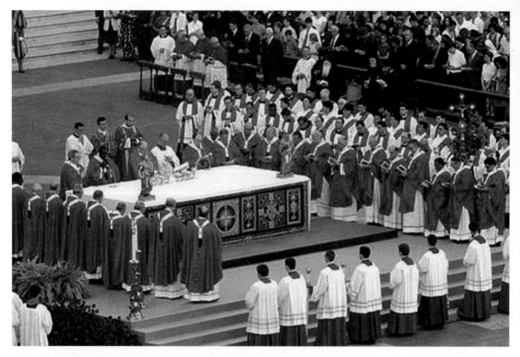

Mass with the Pope after receiving the pallium, St Peter's Square, Rome, 29 June 2002.

A special moment: kneeling to kiss the Pope's ring after receiving the pallium, 29 June 2002.

Helping the 'weans' of St Bernard's Parish celebrate their parish feast day, 18 August 2002.

Visit to Croy, 17 November 2002. With three-week old Louise Glazer, her mother Lynne, grandad Joe Weldon and great-granny Nan Kerr.

A solemn moment: Latin Mass in the Tridentine Rite, 21 September 2002.

The flags are out: the mayor and police chief welcome me to Barga, 9 October 2002.

"I wonder where this leads?" Via dei Conti near Barga, 8 October 2002.

rather than with the Medicean humanists of the high Renaissance!

It was the Rome of Raphael, now indisputably that of Michelangelo, of Giulio Romano, of Vasari, of the architects Della Porta and Maderno (not forgetting Matteo di Castello, the architect of the Chiesa Nuova).

It is the Rome of Pierluigi da Palestrina and the new music. It is the Rome of Vittoria Colonna and her coterie of philosopher-poets, including Michelangelo himself, whose sonnets transcend the sensuality of the high Renaissance using its artistic forms to express the human aspiration for the divine.

It is the Rome of St Ignatius of Loyola and his companions, including the incomparable missionary, Francis Xavier, and the model youth, St Aloysius Gonzaga. It is the Rome of Charles Borromeo and of Robert Bellarmine, of the Roman College, and of the Venerabile (the Venerable English College) and of the oratorium, Baronius, and a new telling of the Church's history.

It is the Rome of Camillus de Lellis and the many who frequented the hospitals; of St John Leonardi, whose work is at the foundation of Propaganda Fide; of the fraternities of Divin' Amore and of the Most Holy Trinity for pilgrims and convalescents; of the nuns of Tor dei Specchi.

It is the Rome of St Felix of Cantalice and of the Franciscan Reform, the Capuchins. It is the Rome where saints greet each other in the street, as do Philip and Felix, extravagantly exchanging hats to the amusement of the bystanders.

It is the Rome where saints write to one another and quarrel for the good of the Church, as do Philip and Charles Borromeo. It is the Rome which sees the painting of the 'Last Judgment' in the Sistine Chapel, and the finishing of St Peter's; the building of the Church of St John of the Florentines, the Gesu' and, of course, the Chiesa Nuova, Philip's own church.

It is the Rome of the palaces built by the noble or ennobled families of the popes, and of the new roads cutting across the city to reveal vistas of the great churches.

It is the Rome of the rediscovery of the catacombs as places of devotion, and where the ancient churches are renewed and re-embellished. It is the Rome of the *Sette Chiese* (the seven ancient basilicas), the combined pilgrimage which is popularised by St Philip and his companions. Well I remember those annual walks when, as a student, I joined a motley group of parishioners of the Chiesa Nuova, friends and Roman seminarians alike, tramping the streets of Rome singing, *'Vanita di vanita: ogni cos'e vanita'* ('Vanity, vanity, all is vanity') to the surprise of the sophisticated, the elegant and the unsuspecting Romans of the 1950s! We sang the verses of the Franciscan poet, Jacopone da Todi, so beloved of St Philip, and our final, foot-weary entrance to the illuminated basilica of Santa Maria Maggiore was like entering the gates of heaven itself.

It is the Rome of the scripture-study and reflection groups, of the prayer confraternities and of the new songs. It is the Rome of the Oratory.

Against the background of all these places and events, in the midst of this great and motley company of saints and sinners, at the heart of this Catholic renewal, is St Philip – the Florentine who made Rome his home; the layman who was persuaded to become a priest; the contemplative who was forced by an inner compulsion – a prompting of the Spirit – to become 'all things to all men'.

He keeps the conscience of Rome, hearing the confessions of high and low alike, stressing, by his actions and apostolate, that the foundation of all reform of the Church is in the personal holiness and integrity of its individual members.

I know I am being self-indulgent in this entry. I am like a traveller to far-away places who must record, for his friends, every detail of his holiday, with photographs and slides – not so much to inform and edify as to share his experience and enthusiasm.

I am taking for granted a knowledge of this lovely saint, of his *affabilita'*, of his gentle wisdom, of his joyful demeanour, of his heart-expanding love of the Lord. In which case, perhaps I am justified in recalling, as I do, the place, the setting and the influence of Philip because I feel as though I am recalling a friend, speaking of one we all love – and there can never be boredom in that – as

Philip might himself have said when speaking of the love of his heart.

Paradoxically, Philip humanised the Rome of the Reform, not by humanist learning and preaching but by his humanity – in caring for the sick, in sharing with the poor, in guiding the consciences of sinners, in warming the hearts of all with marvellous displays of affection, in speaking of the one he loved above all others in terms of the most intimate friendship.

When the reformers of the north were pinning their theses to church doors, writing their institutes and berating their queen, there was placed, in the Eternal City, a friend of God who has not ceased to charm the disciples of Jesus with his Christ-like humanity. Surely in this, at a time of reform – a new reform in the Church – there is a lesson for us all. Movements abound, new forms of the religious life are emerging; the laity are recognising the universal call to holiness as they frequent prayer- and faith-sharing-groups, healing masses and Bible study-programmes. They may still have to rediscover the apostolic warmth of those who minister to them. They have still, by and large, to recover the marvellous balm of the confessional and the value of spiritual direction.

If the sons of St Philip can help in this, they will, as Philip so admirably did, ensure the renewal of the Church.

Friday, 28 June

As I prepare, on this warm and tranquil summer evening at the Pontifical Scots College, for tomorrow's event, my mind drifts back to the years I myself was a student here, from 1952 to 1959.

The Pontifical Scots College in Rome was founded by Pope Clement VIII back in 1600, a jubilee year. Tens of thousands flocked to the city, which once again effectively became the centre of the Catholic world following the conclusion of the Council of Trent and the gradual implementation of its reforms by successive popes and a crop of saints. It was a real moment of hope. At least one of those popes, Pius V, was himself a saint. His tomb is in the beautiful Blessed Sacrament Chapel of the Basilica of Santa Maria Maggiore and it was here, in 1958, that I celebrated mass as a student priest at Christmas.

A few years ago, I wrote a short history of the college. It was a fascinating project. The college was born out of the combined historical circumstances of the Reformation and the Council of Trent. For Scots Catholics, life in the immediate post-Reformation period was far from ideal. The Reformation Parliament had imposed the Protestant profession of faith, banned the mass and forbidden concourse with Rome. There were no Catholic bishops left in the country. Those who did not conform to the new order retired to their fortified palaces to await the abatement of the storm. It never came and they died out one by one.

The last member of this old hierarchy, Archbishop Beaton of Glasgow, wisely delayed his return to Scotland permanently and continued to fulfil a diplomatic role in Paris, first for Mary, Queen of Scots, and then for her son James VI and I. As a student of this history almost half a century ago, it never entered my mind that, one day, I would be called to succeed Beaton in the city of St Mungo – yet here I am! Truly the ways of the Lord are mysterious.

In one way it seems extraordinary that, just when the Catholic Church in Scotland was at its weakest following its sensational institutional collapse in 1560, it should be establishing colleges not only in Rome but also in France, the Netherlands and Spain. Only two of these colleges now remain: the Royal Scots College in Salamanca, which was removed to that city from Valladolid during the last decade having originally been established in Madrid in 1627; and this one – the Pontifical Scots College in Rome.

After the Reformation, journeying abroad for a Catholic education was the only option open to the sons of Catholic gentlemen and those destined for the Catholic priesthood. These foundations would not have taken place had it not been for the efforts and generosity of benefactors abroad, who came to the aid of the ailing and now headless Catholic community.

The Foundation Charter for the Scots College established by Clement VIII did not limit its scope to clerical students. Nonetheless, before two decades were over, it had become, in every respect, a seminary for the training of priests after the model of the Council of Trent. These colleges and religious houses provided the trickle of priests that kept the Catholic faith alive through the so-called 'penal' days. Only with the establishment of the hidden seminary at Scalan in Upper Banffshire in the eighteenth century was there another source of priests for the mission.

The restoration of Catholicism was, in aim and method, both a religious and a political cause. In this, Scotland was no different from the rest of Europe. The principle by which some sort of settlement came was *'cuius regio eius religio'*, which can be loosely translated as 'the religion of a state hinges upon that of its prince'. It was a principle that a clannish Scotland applied. Although, when the clans fought at Culloden, it was ostensibly a political dispute, there is no doubt that the Catholicism and Episcopalianism of certain chiefs and their men had a strong bearing on the side they took. Indeed, our troubles today in Ulster are, I hope, the last European manifestation of this same thing – an unseasonable crop!

The number of students in the college in Rome was never very large and the number of priests produced for the Scottish mission was even smaller, especially in the early years. Numbers, of course, gradually increased as the Church expanded in Scotland and more favourable circumstances allowed easier movement between the countries. They peaked in the 1950s and '60s and, today, there are around a dozen seminarians from Scotland and ten postgraduates from various parts of the world.

As students, our life was not so unlike those of the young men here today or, indeed, of our predecessors. We lived together as a community, sharing the same board, studying philosophy and theology together. In centuries past students attended the Roman College which is now called the Gregorian University. We followed the same rigorous regime of prayers and devotions, and were identified among the many students of other national colleges in Rome by our purple soutanes, crimson sashes and 'sopranos' – black sleeveless outer garments.

The original Scots College was humble in aspect. Old prints show a couple of adjacent houses on the Via Quattro Fontane to which the chapel was attached – built through the generosity of a Marchioness of Huntly in 1645 and still held as the National Church of Catholic Scots in Rome. I visit that old chapel whenever I can – today you need permission from its current owners.

In 1869 the old houses were demolished and replaced by a magnificent new building designed by the architect Luigi Poletti, who was also responsible for rebuilding the Basilica of St Paul Outside the Walls after a disastrous fire earlier in the century. The students moved in in 1870, just when Garibaldi's Risorgimento troops were marching on the city, intent on the unification of Italy and the downfall of the Papal States. And the building's fine façade has not been altered since. The Royal Arms and the Cross of St Andrew continue to adorn it, much to the curiosity of the guests of the Anglo-American hotel opposite and despite the fact that the building is now the prestigious seat of an Italian bank. The students had to flit once again, this time in 1962, to a villa at Marino and then, in 1964, to the new college, so different in style and on the cooler, less frantic fringe of the Eternal City.

The new college is a stylish, modern, red-brick building whose main façade runs parallel to the Via Cassia, with the chapel positioned in between. This too is modern in design, with the roof supported internally by pillars that divide the space into three. The central space forms a well, on each side of which four tiers of benches ascend to the aisles in collegiate fashion. The altar at right angles to these benches is unusually long but in harmony with the space. The table of the altar is carved from white Carrara marble with lips over the sides to give the impression of an altar cloth.

The window space above the altar forms a tympanum, which is filled with the most splendid glass depicting the call of St Andrew and his presentation of the young man with the five barley loaves and two fish from whose meagre picnic lunch the 5000 were fed. This work is by the now famous Hungarian stained-glass artist, Giovanni Hajnal, whose earlier work, undertaken for the College at its formal opening by Pope Paul VI in November 1964, illustrates the Christian history of Scotland and is now one of the treasures of the College.

I have had many happy times both at the old college in the city centre and here, where the current college enjoys a fine position on this ancient Roman road heading north-west towards Tuscany, from where my forebears hail.

Saturday, 29 June

Today is the Feast of Saints Peter and Paul – the day for me to receive the pallium and a day to which I have been looking forward with such great pleasure. On Monday, I was telling my companions of the Order of Malta that I was on my way to Rome for the pallium. One of the ladies replied, 'How awful! It's so cruel. They die like flies.' Well, I know it's hot in Rome – unseasonably hot – but I didn't think it was lethal!

It turned out that she thought I was going out for the Siena Palio, the famous horse race in the piazza of that city – though comparing horses to flies was almost as grotesque as matching archbishops to them! It just goes to show the lack of knowledge of the pallium even among Catholics.

The pallium is a narrow woollen scarf worn round the shoulders, so made that one end hangs down the back and the other on the breast. It is woven from the wool of lambs, blessed earlier in the year on the Feast of St Agnes. The pallium is adorned with six black crosses in silk and appears to be held in place by jewelled pins. Its origin is uncertain but it has been worn over mass vestments by the bishops of Rome and Eastern Churches, since the fourth century, as a badge of their pastoral office. Since the sixth century, it has been conferred by the pope on bishops of the Latin Church and is now normally only conferred on metropolitan archbishops, such as myself, as a symbol of their larger jurisdiction.

I go with Mgr Peter Smith to the Vatican. We are allowed to park our car inside the walls near to the side entrance through which, on presentation of my card, we are ushered in to the Basilica of St

Peter by the ever-courteous Papal Guards. It is undoubtedly one of the world's greatest buildings. Its spaciousness, its harmonious proportions, its marvellous colouring ever delight me. Today it is empty apart from a few officials and the archbishops who are arriving to find, laid out for them on long tables, the vestments they will wear and a box, shaped rather like a little house, in which they will eventually take home their pallium.

I find my place and start to vest. It is very hot this evening and I decide to strip off my red-piped black soutane and sash using Mgr Peter's generous girth – I hope he will forgive me – to cover the operation! I note that, before the mass starts, many will have followed suit!

I find Archbishop Peter Smith, the new Archbishop of Cardiff – with the same name as my colleague – and make an obvious joke about their swapping roles. I meet Archbishop Peter Sarpong from Ghana, who sent me a couple of his priests to help out in Aberdeen when we were both just bishops and I was in need.

In the procession I am next to the new Patriarch of Venice, Archbishop Angelo Scola. I was once in the company of his predecessor, Cardinal Marco Cè, at dinner during a previous plenary of the Joint Working Group held in Venice. He invited me to sit next to him at a performance of Vivaldi's 'Juditha Triumphans' in St Mark's Basilica. I told him how marvellous I thought his cathedral was. 'The finest in the world!' he replied. I believed him that night when it was filled with sound and glittered with light courtesy of Italy's equivalent of Powergen!

As we process out we come into the full glare of the Roman evening sun. We are seated in plush chairs flanking the altar placed on the upper plateau of the great Piazza. The Holy Father moves slowly but deliberately and speaks similarly. To receive the pallium, we each have to mount, in turn, the red-carpeted steps to where he is sitting. It seems a straightforward enough piece of choreography but just you try doing it when you are alone and being watched by tens of thousands in person and millions on TV!

'You are Cardinal Winning's successor,' the Pope says.

JUNE

I am very conscious of that great bond between the Holy See and the Archdiocese of Glasgow, as 'Special Daughter of the Roman Church', when the Holy Father places the pallium over my shoulders. It may seem like a yoke but it is an honour to bear. 'My yoke is easy and my burden is light,' said the Lord. The fact is that a grandson of Italian immigrants, who was brought up in a town close to the Scots faithful of the Enzie of Banffshire and educated by the Irish Sisters of Mercy and the priestly sons of Irish immigrants, now has the honour of representing them all at Rome and of guiding them at home.

I see it as my task as archbishop to remind Glasgow's Catholic faithful of their cultural and spiritual roots. In recent years we have suffered a loss of faith, on the part of those unable to swim against the tide of secularism, and a loss of face, on account of the disgraceful actions of a few. But, despite that, we need to take pride in all that the Church has done and continues to do in the service of the community – not least in the fields of social care and education. I will wear my pallium proudly, albeit with a sense of personal unworthiness.

There is still work to be done. I am appalled at the extent of social and health deprivation in the city. We have to help the disadvantaged to recover their dignity as human beings and rediscover the beauty of fidelity in married life and parenting. We have to offer further opportunities for tertiary education across a wide range of subjects, including those of faith and civic service, and make full use of the ever-increasing advantages of modern technology for learning at home.

Rome and home. These are the poles of my ministry as I presently experience it. For me, the former means our faithful adherence to the Apostolic faith and the special bond we have with the See of Peter – and through it the whole Catholic world. The latter means Glasgow now – its vibrancy as a city, its history as a centre of faith, its inherited social problems and its determination to overcome them. Its motto is sufficient – 'May Glasgow flourish by the preaching of the world and the praising of His name!'

I retreat down the stairs, yoked forever to the person of the Holy Father. For some reason or other it is the picture of my being invested that goes round the world. I have no prouder moment.

Sunday, 30 June

By happy chance, a group of parishioners from Bishopbriggs arranged to come on pilgrimage/holiday to Rome and arrived in the Pontifical Scots College at the very time when I was receiving the pallium yesterday in St Peter's Square. They came under the direction of their curate Mgr Hugh Bradley. He is a former member of the Scots College and an aficionado of Rome, having spent some time as an addetto or assistant at the Congregation for Catholic Education.

For many of them it is their first time in Rome and, for many, it is also the first time they had met with their new archbishop personally. I celebrate mass for them in the College Chapel six months to the day since the phone call that changed my life.

During the course of my homily, I speak of the significance of Rome in terms of understanding the history and culture of Europe. We are not only indebted to the city for much of our architectural inspiration but also for the infrastructure of our cities, the basis of our law and for many words and concepts inherited from its language – Latin.

This beautiful language – the language of philosophers, historians and poets – became the language of the Church, its liturgy and teachings. Even the administration of the Church owes much to the Roman division of areas into dioceses and provinces. Rome, especially during its republican period, was marked by some outstanding human virtues, such as a sense of justice, based upon the establishment and maintenance of law, and a peculiar Roman virtue known as 'pietas'. Whereas we now tend to use the English equivalent, 'piety', to describe private devotions and attachment to the often rather sugary religious objects that we might find on a 'piety stall', the Latin pietas was a robust virtue used to describe the bonds between members of a family and that family's attachment to its household gods.

JUNE

The Gospel of the day presents the difficult passage wherein Jesus says that anyone who prefers their father or mother to Him is not worthy of Him. That said, however, is not to suggest that there is no virtue in the strong affection we express in family relationships, but that the virtue of pietas necessarily binds us to Him first, in whose image we were made and through whose humanity we are saved. Afterwards one of the staff tells me that he overheard a member of my new archdiocese declaring as he left the chapel: 'He fairly knows his stuff!'

July

If the group of parishioners from Bishopbriggs benefited in some way from our Roman encounter – and certainly, for me, their presence was an immense pleasure – they also benefited in another way. They become my 'entourage' this morning when the Holy Father gives a special audience to the new archbishops and those who are with them in Rome.

I am able to present seven people to the Holy Father, including two ladies who have given outstanding service to the Church in Scotland and who were members of the archdiocese: Mrs Maureen Byrne, former National President of the Union of Catholic Mothers, and Miss Agnes Malone, for some time Director of Social Services for the Archdiocese and now Director of the Scottish Children's Hospice.

To allow us to stay for this special audience, Mgr Peter Smith has managed to change our flight tickets. Nevertheless, we need to leave the audience hall before the Holy Father who is still greeting people at his seat.

Mgr Peter and I try to sneak out, using a side aisle, only to be ushered back towards the main one. I hear clapping and cheering and turn to see what the Holy Father has done to deserve it, only to realise that the noise was none other than Bishopbriggs saying goodbye to its archbishop.

We skulk away as quickly as we can!

We arrived back in Glasgow in time for me to meet the group from the archdiocese which is preparing for the International Youth Gathering with the pope in Toronto. My driver, Gerry Beechey's wife, Helen, is with them in the Eyre Hall with a group from their home parish. Since I have my case with me, I dress for them as I did for the pope (why not?) and show them the pallium – in its little house!

July

Tuesday, 2 July – Wednesday 3 July

I journey alone by car up the A90 from Perth to Inverness for Mgr Robert McDonald's Golden Jubilee of Priesthood. For many years, he was the diocesan treasurer in Aberdeen and, therefore, a close colleague. Mgr Robert has also been a good friend and a regular holiday companion over the years and I am delighted to preside at a mass in St Mary's, celebrated by the clergy of the diocese, and to propose a toast to the jubilarian at a meal thereafter in a local hotel.

Thursday, 4 July

A joyful day at Pluscarden Abbey in nearby Moray, close to my home town. I ordain Tony Schmitz, the Director of the Ogilvie Institute, to the permanent diaconate. My personal satisfaction is not only in seeing a good friend achieve his ambition but in recognising that, in him, two of my own endeavors come together – namely the restoration in Aberdeen of the permanent diaconate and the foundation of the Ogilvie Institute as an agency of faith development in conjunction with the Maryvale Institute in Birmingham, which uses the distance-learning mode in its education programming.

In the evening, Mgr Robert and I are honoured by the Abbot and community of Pluscarden in what they call a *'Gaudeamus'* (literally, 'let us rejoice'). It is great to see this body of men, whose lives are entirely dedicated to the Benedictine ideal of prayer and work (*ora et labora*), enjoying some innocent fun with songs and sketches – occasionally at one another's expense – while consuming sticky buns, boxes of chocolates, beer and Coke in front of the great fireplace of the Chapter Room. This vaulted chamber, with its central column, would have been at the heart of the social and administrative life of the medieval abbey and must have witnessed many a conversation of its abbots and monks as they reflected on the vicissitudes of their time.

After the silence of the centuries, the Abbey was reopened in 1948 and has resounded to the voices of devoted men ever since.

Tonight, it peals with innocent laughter – what a wonderful sound.

Friday, 5 July

I'm dictating this in the garden of Pluscarden Abbey at 3 o'clock in the afternoon. For a change it's pleasant enough to be sitting out – cloudy but with moments of sunshine and a gentle, if somewhat cool, breeze.

Tomorrow I go to Tynet and then on to Portsoy to celebrate Fr Ronnie Walls' silver jubilee. He was the first priest I ordained when I became Bishop of Aberdeen. And then it's on to Scalan for the annual mass at the old seminary in Upper Banffshire. It was at Scalan in the eighteenth century that one hundred priests were trained and ordained for the Scottish mission. Arguably, the survival of the Catholic Church in Scotland would not have been secure without that hidden seminary and the work of its teachers, such as George Hay, who had been educated in Rome and who subsequently was ordained bishop in that remote farmhouse in the Banffshire hills. A convert from Episcopalianism, Bishop Hay became a priest in Rome at the age of twenty-nine, a bishop at forty and died at Aquhorties in 1811 at the age of eighty-two. He was vicar apostolic of the lowland district of Scotland, the area east and south of what might be called the Highland line stretching from Dumbarton in the south-west to Nairn on the Moray Firth.

It was the attachment to the Catholic faith by people in remote areas of the country, such as this, that ensured that the Church continued throughout the darkest penal days and who, therefore, provided that precious thread of continuity that binds the Catholic Church of today to the Church of Ninian, Columba, Margaret and John Ogilvie and the many other Scottish saints, some of whom I had the privilege of having depicted on the lateral chancel walls of the cathedral in Aberdeen. If one lead from Glasgow takes us into the many parts of Ireland from which so many immigrants came in the late eighteenth and nineteenth centuries, the other lead takes us to the lands of Banffshire, to the west Highlands and

July

Western Isles of Scotland. It is on these intertwined threads, like the woven green and gold cord on which hangs the bishop's pectoral cross, that the Church in Glasgow depends on historically.

After Scalan I go to Aberdeen, where I will be arranging my final 'flit'. These days are full of emotion and nostalgia.

Friday, 12 July – Thursday, 18 July
I leave early on this Friday morning for Prestwick where I join sick and able pilgrims en route for Lourdes. Last year I stood at the edge of the crowd – our Aberdeen pilgrimage overlapping with Glasgow's. This year I am in the thick of it. As always, it is a deeply satisfying experience.

For me, the high point is presiding at the blessing of the sick in the underground basilica filled with thousands of pilgrims from all over the world. I am flanked by the bonnie lassies of the St Margaret of Scotland Lourdes Group in their white shirts and tartan sashes and by the handsome lads of the same group carrying incense braziers. I feel immensely proud to be associated with them. To see the imploring eyes of countless people turned towards the monstrance (the display vessel in which the consecrated host is carried) with which I trace the sign of the cross over them is also humbling.

For the rest, I carry my candle, I drink the water, I bathe in the waters of the baths and I pray – as all do with evident ease at Lourdes. And, for the first time in years, I play cards in the evening – and win! (Due, I hasten to add, to luck, not prayer!)

Friday, 19 July
We leave Glasgow for Toronto today to attend World Youth Day with Pope John Paul II – 'we' being the 140 fellow travellers from Glasgow and the forty-six from Aberdeen. I am booked in with the latter since arrangements for my accompanying the group had already been made prior to my transfer to Glasgow. In the end the Aberdeen group is put on an earlier plane and we fly with Air Canada.

After a seven-hour flight we arrive early in the afternoon, local time, at Toronto. At the airport there, we await the arrival of other parties, which include groups from Argyll and the Isles with Bishop Ian Murray, from St Andrews and Edinburgh under the leadership of Archbishop Keith O'Brien and one from Galloway, which is without its bishop since he has had to undergo hospital treatment. Other groups from Scottish dioceses come from Motherwell, Paisley and Dunkeld.

The archdiocesan group travel separately to London Ontario, the diocese where they will spend the weekend billeted with families, while the Aberdeen, Argyll and Galloway groups are together at a hall of residence of the University of Western Ontario.

Sunday, 21 July

Those billeted with families have a marvellous experience. Staying at the university has proved, I think, to be the less attractive option. It has meant that we have not had the advantage of contact with local people nor, indeed, the local parish since the chaplaincy of the university is separate and most of our activities are taking place in the grounds of St Peter's Seminary, one of two major seminaries in the area.

The weather is very hot and there has been a great deal of walking to be done – quite demanding, given the unaccustomed climatic conditions!

Monday, 22 July

I have moved with our groups to Oakview University accommodation, which is certainly much more comfortable and within easier reach of the centre of the city. There is, however, a gathering for all those who have been hosted during the weekend in the dioceses of Ontario. On the hottest day of the summer we find ourselves crossing a drought-blighted field and sitting exposed to the merciless rays of the sun while we hear the stories of the Canadian saints and early Christian pioneers. It is there that I meet up with some sections of the Glasgow party. We are all feeling somewhat exhausted, dusty and travel weary. The sun beats down mercilessly and the wind rises creating a dust bowl, before eventually heavy clouds come across and there is a downpour, by which time we are fortunately in or within reach of our hundred or so buses. Never was a shower so greatly appreciated by so many!

Tuesday, 23 July

We all gather again, this time with tens of thousands of other young pilgrims at the Exhibition Place in downtown Toronto. Again this is a hot day and any form of shade is avidly sought. The Cardinal Archbishop of Toronto, Aloysius Ambrosic, presides.

For all of us, it is the first taste of the scale of the youth gathering. Parties of exuberant young people, colourfully dressed and proudly carrying their national flags, make their way to and fro finding their position in the grounds or streaming out afterwards to find their way home.

It is a memorable day, not least because it began with a trip to Niagara Falls. Quite magnificent.

Thursday, 25 July

The last three days have been set aside for catechesis on the theme: 'You are the salt of the earth; you are the light of the world'. I have agreed to act as a bishop catechist and am initially assigned to the parish of the Merciful Redeemer, whose new church building is very beautiful and whose congregation of young people is very enthusiastic. Here are the thoughts I share with them.

'You are the light of the world. A city set on a hill cannot be hidden. Let your light shine before men in such a way that they may see your good works, and glorify your Father who is in heaven' (Matt. 5: 14).

Let me tell you something about myself. For twenty-five years I was Bishop of Aberdeen in the north-east of Scotland. On 17 June last year Cardinal Winning, Archbishop of Glasgow, died suddenly; on 29 December I was told that the Holy Father had nominated me to replace him – Cardinal Winning, that is!

It has been all go ever since! And much of the 'go' has been outside of the archdiocese since I already had a programme of events as Bishop of Aberdeen which I had to honour – including my silver jubilee as a bishop – and I inherited a programme of events as well, including leading the archdiocesan pilgrimage to Lourdes from which I returned the day before I came here. (When I couldn't get my case closed, I realised I had put clean linen in without removing the old!)

I have truly been a Roaming Catholic – or a phantom archbishop – in recent weeks!

At Lourdes I was press-ganged into singing a song at the Ceilidh for the sick. When I saw how readily the young people were giving of their best, I could not refuse! But I got my own back – in a sort of way – by singing the following well-known Scots music hall song:

When I was a child, a tiny wee child,
My mother said to me,
'Come see the Northern Lights, my child,
They're bright as they can be.'
She called them the heavenly dancers,
Merry dancers in the sky.
I'll never forget that wonderful sight,
They made the heavens bright.

Chorus
Oh the Northern Lights of Old Aberdeen
Mean home sweet home to me.
The Northern Lights of Old Aberdeen
Are what I long to see.
I've been a wand'rer all of my life
And many's a sight I've seen.
Godspeed the day

July

When I'm on my way
To my home in Aberdeen.

The phenomenon referred to in this song is called the Aurora Borealis, literally the 'Northern Dawn'. It is an extremely beautiful sight – rays of coloured light flash or dance across the northern sky – the 'merry dancers'.

I remember, as a student in Rome, climbing in the dark up Monte Cavo near the Holy Father's summer residence in what are called the Castelli Romani to see the dawn race across the Roman *campagna*. Within a very short period of time, the darkness was dispelled – beautiful, golden light gently bathed the vineyards and rolling plain of the countryside around Rome and eventually I could see it reflected on the dome of St Peter's in the far distance.

How beautiful is the dawn – it is the birth of a new day – it is a symbol of hope.

Even the false dawn of the Northern Lights is a harbinger of light, telling us that the sun is shining where we cannot see it – reflecting off the northern snows. Like the moon rising, not the source of light, but a reflection of it.

I want to return to Lourdes. There is a short passage in the latest edition of the *Lourdes* magazine telling of what happened at Lourdes and its significance. A strange adventure!

Below the little town of Lourdes in the French Pyrenees, on the morning of Thursday, 11 February 1858, a poor little girl went down to gather wood on the edge of a river. Suddenly, in a grotto, she received the sweet visit of a 'young lady' of light who appeared in the crevice of a rock. Later, the truth came out: it was the Virgin Mary who appeared to her!

What a strange adventure this child had. Her name was Bernadette Soubirous. At the time of her vision, she didn't know how to read or write but she had a lot of common sense and loved Jesus and Mary more than anything! People from around the world heard about her story of faith and prayer.

131

Today, multitudes of people come from the four corners of the world. About 6 million people come to Lourdes every year to deepen their faith and to find comfort when life becomes difficult. Lourdes is a place of light! There you can receive Jesus' love which he gives continuously in service to others, in communion, adoration and the sacrament of forgiveness! In Lourdes, more than a century ago, God trusted a child who was a lot like you. God is calling you, just as he called Bernadette, to be a ray of sunshine to those around you.

I saw that ray of sunshine in Lourdes in the group of young boys and girls who accompanied the sick – the St Margaret of Scotland Youth Group. They made me a member – gave me this cap – and so I was qualified to join the youth in Toronto!

They wheeled the sick in their *voitures*. They fetched food and drink for them. They spoke and prayed with them. They showed them love and sang them songs and they enjoyed themselves hugely. And so they deserved to carry bowls of incense in the Blessed Sacrament Procession – the boys in their white shirts and kilts and the girls in their whites with tartan sashes, carrying torches and banners.

I was immensely proud of them, as I am of you!

Jesus said: 'You are the light of the world' (you are to reflect Christ who is the light). 'Let your light shine before men in such a way that they may see your good works and glorify your Father who is in heaven' (Matt. 5: 13–14).

Light illuminates and warms – the light in our hearts is that of charity, of love by which we warm the lives of others. That light is truly a reflection of Christ who is, in St John's words, the light of life.

All things came into being through Him and apart from Him nothing came into being that has come into being. In Him was life and the life was the light of men – the light shines in the darkness and we saw his glory, glory as of the only begotten from the Father, full of grace and truth. (John 1: 3, 4, 14)

July

I am content with the catechesis. My hope and prayer is that the young people will find some food for thought, some inspiration which might encourage them on their pilgrim way.

Friday, 26 June

Today I am taken to a parish nearer the centre of Toronto that is dedicated to St Anselm. Here I have to catechise on the theme of 'Be reconciled to God'.

Our theme today is 'reconciliation' and it is part of an extended catechesis which the Holy Father has not only suggested, but which he himself has addressed – as we heard yesterday when we greeted him and he greeted us.

First we had the theme of 'salt of the earth' and we recalled the words Jesus addressed to his disciples: 'You are the salt of the earth'. Our Holy Father commented last August:

> One of the main functions of salt is to season food, to give it taste and flavour. Through baptism, our whole being has been profoundly changed because it has been seasoned with the new life from Christ. The salt that keeps our Christian identity intact, even in a very secularised world, is the grace of baptism. As the salt of the earth, you are called to preserve the faith which you have received and to pass it on intact to others. Your generation is being challenged in a special way to keep safe the deposit of faith, i.e., what has been handed down to you.

Those who are engaged with young people, especially in their teenage years – I mean teachers, pastors, youth leaders – know how strong peer pressure can be. By that we mean the influence of the whole group on individuals – on the way they dress, the music they buy, the food they eat, the sort of recreation and socialising they apparently enjoy. It is like a river – we can no longer identify the streams which have fed it – the water flows in one lot.

But, for the individual who sees that the course is not what he or she wants to follow, it can be very difficult to withstand the pressure. It is like swimming against the current. But there may be times when being faithful to oneself – to what one has received – to Christ – makes it is necessary to swim against the stream.

Here in Toronto, the counter-current of young people who want to follow Christ is very strong. Here is a company of Christians who, encouraged by one another, can withstand the pressures of the world to conform to its standards and, instead, to follow Christ – to live lives of integrity, purity, generosity of heart, honesty, and to experience the joy of so-doing.

The Holy Father remarks:

> In this secularised age when many of our contemporaries think and act as if God did not exist or are attracted to material forms of religion, it is you, dear young people, who must show that faith is a personal decision, which involves your whole life.

I then go on to explain how the Mission to the Arctic Regions – or the Vicariate of the North Pole, as it was also called – had been set up by a group of Flemish missionaries in what is now the parish of St Joachim's and St Anne's in Caithness in the mid-1800s. They had been given the task of bringing the Catholic faith, not only to the people of the local area and the northern islands of Scotland, but also to a wide missionary territory that extended from Hudson Bay in Northern Canada to Greenland, Iceland, the Faroe Islands and Lapland at the very north of Norway within the Arctic Region.

I had been parish priest there for nearly fifteen years and it was during this time that I came across an account of the missionary endeavours of these pioneering priests.

Among the stories they told was that of one of their number arriving on the isles of Orkney. He had barely got there when

someone asked him to visit a woman some distance away. When
he arrived, he found that she was dying but had always
harboured the hope of becoming a Catholic. He was able to
receive her into the Church – to reconcile her on her deathbed.
He marvelled at the providence of God and remarked: 'God
would send an angel if necessary to bring even one soul to safety
in God's arms.'

Our theme is reconciliation – our being ambassadors for
Christ. Reconciliation means basically our return to God. Our
very baptism is a form of reconciliation since we are all born
with tendencies towards self, selfishness, sin.

The Spirit of God is given to us as the principle of the Christ-
life in us. When Jesus entered on his public ministry, it was with
the words: 'Repent – turn to God – for the Kingdom of Heaven is
close at hand' (Mark 1: 5).

But reconciliation is an ongoing task – we ever have a need to
repent, to turn to God anew. The sacrament of reconciliation
provides us with the opportunity of forever returning to the
Lord.

I was at Lourdes recently. I decided to go to confession and I
went to what had previously been the hospital, now fitted out as
a chapel of reconciliation. I joined a queue and, in due course,
my turn came.

It is always more difficult for a priest – even worse for a
bishop – to have a face-to-face with a fellow priest! Despite the
circumstances, the confessor offered me a passage of scripture. It
was the following: 'I do not call you servants any more, I call
you friends because I have made known to you everything I
have learnt from my father' (John 15: 15). Providentially, I had
need of that passage later at a holy hour in the hospital and I
recall it now as we reflect on the theme of reconciliation for,
having been reconciled ourselves, we are sent to be ambassadors
of Christ's peace.

An ambassador is one who knows his prince's mind – who is
privy to his purposes, who is ready to advocate his cause. And

we, says St Paul, are ambassadors for Christ. 'It is,' he says, 'as though God were making an appeal through us' and gives us our message: 'We beg you on behalf of Christ – be reconciled to God.'

Among the comments thereafter is one from a young American fellow who says how much he needs to kneel in front of a priest – someone like himself – to confess his sins – it teaches him humility!

Afterwards I am able to celebrate mass – and how appropriately it is the feast of St Joachim and St Anne, the patrons of my Caithness parish!

At the Colony Hotel, in downtown Toronto, I am meeting many colleagues, some old friends and acquaintances and some new contacts. We exchange experiences of these catechism sessions and I think I would be right in saying that all of us have found them a very positive part of the programme.

Of course, it isn't all prayer and catechism. Much fun is had by the young people as they make friends and share jokes and experiences. Their joy is infectious!

Saturday, 27 July

I record these thoughts as I await the bus that will take the assembled cardinals, archbishops and bishops from Toronto's downtown Colony Hotel to Downsview Lands for the first of the two events with which the World Youth Day will conclude.

Tonight, at 7.30 p.m., there will be solemn vespers in the presence of the Holy Father who has been resting at Strawberry Island, a lakeside venue north of Toronto. Last night he was seen on television watching the magnificent *Way of the Cross*, a dramatised re-enactment of the crucifixion, that he himself had composed for a similar event in Rome during Holy Week of the Jubilee Year. During each of the fourteen stations placed at intervals up Toronto's magnificent University Avenue, Canadian actors portrayed the scenes of Our Lord's Passion. Tens of thousands of young people and others from Toronto and beyond attended and were deeply moved by the beauty of the portrayal, by the profound reflections of the Holy Father and the uplifting song of the accompanying choirs. I don't think anyone who was present last night will ever forget the experience.

There have been other experiences, of course, which I for one will not forget – experiences that have not been so emotional but memorable as acts of survival. I think, in particular, of that drought-affected field on the hottest day of the year right at the start – moments when I thought that this, the first, would also be the last of my World Youth Days! Of course, I imagine that, for the young people who have been so resilient, the hardships have been less than those felt by a sixty-eight-year-old. However, now that I am ensconced with most of the bishops in a downtown hotel, my memories of hardship are somewhat eased and an inclination towards sharing such events in the future, should the Lord allow it, has grown.

Certainly the experience has been tremendous and mainly on account of the exuberance of the young people, both our own and the many others we have met. Their friendliness and evident devotion show that, when good Catholic young people come together and feel supported by one another and led well – as they have been by the dedicated adults, youth leaders and hopefully bishops – they respond so well. Our hope must surely be that, from so many, some vocations to the priesthood or religious life will emerge.

But it is more than hope. It is real expectation that those who have participated this week will be among the most robust of our Catholic laity in the future.

August

Thursday, 1 August

I'm home again and back to work at Clyde Street, next to the cathedral. The cathedral is the mother church. It may not be the first church in historical terms, nor the most distinguished architecturally, but it is first insofar as it contains the seat or 'cathedra' of the bishop. In the case of Glasgow, however, St Andrew's was, in fact, historically the first church building to be erected after the Reformation for the then-growing Catholic population and, therefore, enjoys historical pre-eminence too.

One of the foremost architects of the day, James Gillespie Graham, designed the building and this ensures its architectural as well as its historical significance. On completion in 1816, it was said to be the most spacious and finest Catholic church in the British Isles – a distinction which it rapidly lost when, following Catholic emancipation in 1829, a great building programme was put in motion. This led to the building of such distinguished churches as St Chad's in Birmingham, consecrated in 1841, and, of course, Westminster Cathedral in London, consecrated in 1910.

Over the summer, however, I have watched a twelve-storey block of flats grow next to our car park on Clyde Street – first digging down into an excavated basement and then, scaffold by scaffold, frame upon frame, steel beams being put in place until the building soars above the offices.

I view this monstrosity with ever growing amazement. How could the council and their planners have changed the rules to allow this building to tower over its neighbours and alter the roof line of the other buildings coasting this section of the Clyde, destroying the pinnacle profile of the cathedral as seen from the Kingston Bridge.

The archdiocesan offices, built in 1988, were not allowed to extend to five floors. Instead, they measured up to the same height as the next-door cathedral and, being faced with reflective glass, mirrored its well-articulated buttressed and pinnacled flank. During all this time, our car park – the one through which I made my surreptitious entry to the offices in January – has been reduced to half its size by the crane used for this obtrusive building.

Friday, 16 August

I get a call at home. Ronnie Convery informs me that the *Sunday Herald* is very keen to have a statement from me on the current tension vis-à-vis Iraq.

Earlier in the week a petition organised by *Pax Christi*, a Christian peace group, caused a stir. It denounced UK and US policy on Iraq and was signed by many churchmen and women. I wasn't asked to sign it and I doubt whether I could have. My own feeling is that denunciations of allied foreign policy could be quite counter-productive – inadvertently offering succour to the brutal regime of Saddam Hussein and encouraging him in his folly.

Eventually I agree to make the following statement.

Diplomatic efforts are, by their very nature, discreet and involve trying to build the largest possible alliance of nations so as to bring pressure on Saddam Hussein to halt his development of chemical, biological and possibly nuclear weapons.

Military strategies, on the other hand, are marked by a degree of sabre-rattling and tough talking – the aim, presumably, being to compel the Iraqi regime to be more forthcoming in its dealings with the international community and more humane in its treatment of its own people.

As a bishop, I do not claim any special insight into either the diplomatic or military strategies. It is easier to express a hope than an opinion, and that hope is that these strategies will succeed in compelling Saddam Hussein to respond to world opinion.

As an ambassador of Christ's peace, it is clear to me that going to war must only ever be regarded as the very last resort –

a step which could be justified only when every other avenue had been explored. My prayer is that a solution will be achieved without resort to this fearful step.

Monday, 26 August

Yesterday the *Sunday Herald* published a listing of Scotland's 150 most influential people. I was interested and read it, hoping I wouldn't appear. I did. I'm the only churchman listed and probably the oldest person to have an entry!

To some extent, I suppose, as holder of this office I am unlikely to escape this kind of attention. Yet, as I read it, I am fascinated to work out what common threads there might be among those listed. Equally interesting is the question of why some prominent church leaders are not included.

The Church needs dialogue with the many other realms of society. I am encouraged to think seriously about instigating meetings and receptions where we can come face-to-face with one another and share something of the wisdom and experience of the Catholic Church.

I'm also asked today to speak about bigotry. The *Glasgow Evening Times* carried a story about a survey in which 12 per cent of people say they have personal experience of bigotry at work and two-thirds say tension between Catholics and Protestants is still a significant problem. I immediately recalled the incident a couple of weeks ago when a can of white paint was thrown across my driveway – my first personal experience of bigotry since I arrived in Glasgow. I am tempted to mention this in my answer to the newspaper, but both Ronnie and Mgr Peter Smith urge caution, fearing that such a revelation might draw attention to my address and unwittingly provoke follow-ups.

I take their advice and respond as follows.

The more the press does to expose the imbecilic behaviour of a small minority of bigots, the sooner we shall be able to live in peace.

The Church is committed to eradicating the cancer of sectarianism from society. I had been forewarned about sectarianism before coming to Glasgow and I have seen evidence of naked sectarian bigotry in the graffiti on the streets. More worrying are cases like that of the parish priest whose church and house were bombarded with petrol bombs. This phenomenon also has a hidden but very damaging effect on people's lives when they are so fearful that they cannot go out in the evenings.

Of course, this kind of hooliganism is not unique to Glasgow. In other places it has a different focus – for example, racism. In Glasgow groups of hooligans have used and abused religious labels to justify their behaviour. They give the impression that genuine Catholic and Protestant people are totally divided – yet, where there is genuine religious commitment, this is not the case.

Their other tactic has been to hijack the honest sporting endeavours of the city's great football clubs and use these as a cover for acts of mindless hooliganism.

This survey simply shows the need for greater determination to stamp out bigotry. Through our schools and parishes we constantly preach the message of fairness and justice for all people, irrespective of colour or creed, and we have a very special concern for anyone who has been ill-treated, abused or discriminated against because of their religion.

The call to treat our fellow human beings with care and justice is one of the cornerstones of the Christian message. Those who practise sectarianism and promote bigotry should realise that their activities are not only unjust, they are abhorrent to Christian sentiment and tradition.

Friday, 30 August

Here I am at the end of another week! During the summer months I have a fairly regular routine. After mass in my oratory and breakfast, Mgr Peter Smith, the Chancellor who lives nearby, picks me up and we motor in to the offices in Clyde Street. The route we take both coming and going has been hallowed by tradition. My predecessor would have no deviation from the course: by Langside, under the walls of the Carmelite monastery in Mansionhouse Road, past the Victoria Infirmary where my predecessor died, skirting Queen's Park, through Crosshill and into the Gorbals – gradually being reinhabited – across the bridge and into Clyde Street and the small car park hedged between the offices and that huge new block of flats.

There are several advantages in these daily journeys to the office. For one thing, I can observe Glaswegians in their native habitat. For another, I can gradually learn the lingo. I mean the new vocabulary – words like 'tumshie', 'howff' and 'nyaff', which an observant ear learns to connect to various people and places, real or anticipated, moving vehicles and pedestrians, and nearly always to road planners in some far from mythical local authority office! When I left Caithness to become archbishop, I was given paperweights. When I came to Glasgow, I was given books on the patter – and *parliamo* Glasgow. Both in their own way seemed appropriate.

Arriving in the offices, the pattern is the same each day: a brief hello to Eileen at the desk; a swift engagement of the lift where inevitably we meet staff on their way to the kitchen for the first, second or third cup of coffee of the day; pay our respects in passing to Sister Veronica, the vice-chancellor; and take up residence in our adjacent offices.

Mine has lovely views up and down the river and across to the splendid row of Georgian houses on the south bank on Carlton Place, next to the new courts that have been designed to match in height the adjacent buildings. Further to the south-east, on the edge of the Gorbals, I can see the Glasgow Mosque with its elegant minaret, topped with the crescent and star of the Muslim faith.

After opening my case in the never fulfilled hope of emptying it, Mgr Peter enters with the latest correspondence, matters arising and the programme for the day. Unless a not-to-be-missed appointment intervenes, this means interviews with two priests, one at a time, before lunch, and the same after it, all four joining me in the dining room for a meal.

What I have lost, above all, in my move to Glasgow is the company and friendship of the priests of the Diocese of Aberdeen, and the many parishioners throughout the whole of that vast area and members of religious orders, both male and female, whom I came to know over the years and whose hospitality I have enjoyed. In compensation, however, I am truly blessed with six times as many priests in Glasgow and, as yet, an unknown number of religious and, of course, many, many more lay people.

I cannot overstate how much I have valued my conversations with these priests since being in Glasgow and how impressed I have been at their courtesy, frankness and remarkable dedication to the people whom they have been appointed to serve. I cannot imagine any bishop in this country or elsewhere being able to boast of them as I can after the interviews I have had over recent months. What they have shown me and this was intended, of course, is my need of them and – can I say this without creating a false impression? – their need of me. A bishop, without his priests, is useless and a body of priests, without the linking and leading of their own shepherd, can lack direction or feel unsupported in their endeavours. I am certainly now one of their own and I want to be available to them whenever they need me.

If the priests appear to appreciate the opportunities that this programme of interviews has provided, I certainly have. I have been able to gauge the concerns of each priest and their expectations. And I have been able to build up a picture of the archdiocese, its strengths and its weaknesses, helped by the extended maps of it set up for me by Mgr Peter on boards borrowed from the RE department and spread all over the room: the city centre parishes near at hand; Cumbernauld and the eastern periphery of the archdiocese at one end of the room; and Dunbartonshire opposite, embracing Loch Lomond. I have had a certain amount of amusement watching priests trying to find their parishes, sometimes confusing the motorway with the river with disastrous results and sometimes having to work their way, parish by parish, from the centre or from the outer edges. I mentally award them marks, the sort I used to give to passengers for the length of time they took to find and get fixed into the car's seat belt. I think of this when I too get into a fankle (I think that's Glaswegian!) in somebody else's vehicle. Truth to tell we always find our way eventually. No phantom parish was noted and no name lost of the 106 that make up the city and its immediate environs.

What strikes me about the description of the parishes that priests give me is the frequent reference to areas of urban deprivation – not in any one part of the city but north, south, east and west, often cheek by jowl with areas of prosperity. No example is more telling than that of Drumchapel and Bearsden, connected, as they are, by a narrow road that skirts up the edge of a wooded hill, once a bastion on the Roman Antonine Wall. You enter the leafy suburb of Bearsden by Chesters Road (named after the Roman camp) on which we have, perhaps appropriately, the National Senior Seminary, or College, for the training of our priests. In social terms, these two areas of the city are worlds apart.

Throughout this period I have been visiting parishes, apparently on a haphazard basis but, in truth, these visits are made to coincide with their patronal feasts. The very first such visit was to St John Ogilvie's, Easterhouse, a fine and commodious church on high ground dignifying the somewhat run-down scheme.

The priest there has had his garage burned down by vandals, has had been verbally abused even on his own property and has had to cut down some of his trees as they gave cover to stone-throwing youngsters whose antics necessitated the erection of wire-mesh protection on many of the windows of both the church and the house.

I was particularly welcomed there on my unexpected visit by the parishioners. They had suffered the bereavement of their former priest – his death having been caused, many believe, by the intolerable level of harassment he had been subjected to. The new priest let it be known that he had quite a few brothers. He heard someone say: 'Better leave that f****** priest alone – he's got seven f****** brothers!' Hardly the reason one expects in a civilised society for desisting from gratuitous attacks on property and persons!

So often, the priests have mentioned people's fear of going out at night, the sense of intimidation they feel and the vandalism and many sorts of vulgarity they experience. If we add to this anecdotal evidence the more scientifically obtained statistics on violence and sectarian strife, as well as poor health, drug addiction and alcoholism, we have the darker side of a picture wherein we see, in greater relief, the sturdy devotion of so many faithful members of the Church and the tenacity of their piety. Many parts of the city are areas of social deprivation. The greatest deprivations of all, however, are the cultural and spiritual ones that undoubtedly result in part from endemic poverty, but must also be related to the loss of the sense of community values, to the loss of faith or its practice. This, I know, I have to face.

One of the effects of this intimidating behaviour, on the streets and closes in some parts of the city, is the reluctance of people, especially older people, to go out at nights. This affects badly the archdiocese's plan to set up and promote neighbourhood groups – groups intended to allow neighbours to share faith, reflect on its import and take it out into the community: community building on the basis of faith and its commandment of practical love of neighbour and itself. People are inhibited by the lack of that neighbourliness and solidarity once famously connected with the 'stairheeds' of the Gorbals tenements.

In many parishes the parish hall has become the 'stairheed'. I recall one visit to St Mungo's, Townhead, where the hall on one level was receiving bus loads of the lonely elderly and on another mothers and toddlers from the refugee community boxed into flats in nearby Sighthill. Not a few of the Glasgow parishes are catering for refugees, even inviting them to mass. At St Bernard's, Nitshill, many came forward at communion time for a blessing. I asked one individual, 'Catholic?' 'Kurdish,' he replied.

In addition, the Missionaries of Charity (Mother Theresa's order) brought with them a crowd of 'street urchins', as they call them. Never did I see a buffet disappear so quickly in the inverted order of sweet things first! Which reminds me of an incident during my visit to Our Lady of the Assumption parish in Ruchill. At a certain point in the queue to greet me at the end of mass, there was a crowd of smallish boys.

'What are your names?' I asked.

'Jason, Craig and Billy.'

It did cross my mind that they were strikingly deficient in saints' names. Anyway, they brought scraps of paper to get my autograph – a practice started further up the line by a pious granny or two. So I stretched out a hand towards a neighbouring table and collected some extra mass books, which I duly inscribed with their impious names and a blessing.

'You know who I am?' I asked.

'Yes,' ventured one. 'Fr Lyons!' Fr Lyons is the parish priest.

'No,' I said, 'I am your new archbishop.' They looked a little nonplussed.

I later remarked to Mgr Peter that I had not even noticed them during mass. 'Of course not,' he said, 'they were just kids playing outside on their bikes who saw that something was going on and hoped for a scramble!' A 'scramble' is a wedding custom which has almonds as its prime matter in Italy, paper confetti (Italian for sweets) at posh weddings in Britain and loose change in Glasgow. The thought of these youngsters possibly returning to their bemused parents with mass books inscribed by the archbishop gave me as much amusement as concern!

September

Another hurdle has been crossed, further progress made in the process of becoming, not just in name but also in effect, the Archbishop of Glasgow. I have my first meeting with the College of Consultors.

During a vacancy at a diocese when there is no archbishop around, the organs of consultation on which he depends are naturally no longer required and, therefore, cease to exist. So the Council of Priests goes on hold, as do any other such consultative bodies set in place by a previous bishop, waiting to be revived by the new one. Indeed, the Code of Canon Law requires that, within a year, any new bishop should establish a new Council of Priests and approve its statutes.

The one body that does, however, continue, in order to provide that necessary continuity between one episcopate and the next and ensure the proper administration of the diocese during a vacancy, is the College of Consultors. It is drawn from the Council of Priests and, since this has 'about half' of its members 'freely elected' by the priests of the diocese, you could say that an element of democracy is present within the structures of the Church.

While it would be possible for a bishop to choose all the members of a College of Consultors from his own appointees to the Council of Priests, in practice, such a college is made up of both the bishop's nominees and those elected by the clergy. It would not be prudent to act otherwise. The virtue of prudence is essential and is presumed to be present in every bishop. Indeed, it is one of the qualities required of a man who is regarded as suitable for the leadership of a diocese.

Except in a few circumstances, well defined in Canon Law where the consent of the College of Consultors is required, it is still possible for a bishop to act arbitrarily. But, while consent is

147

generally not required, consultation is. It would be an imprudent bishop who, having consulted and heard overwhelmingly from those appointed to be his advisors that a course of action was not desirable, acted contrary to such advice.

One could say that the monarchical principle is stronger than the democratic here but, when prudence is added into the equation, it is unlikely that decisions made by a bishop are without the support of his clergy. Those who advise him know that their opinion and judgement must be based upon good reason. For it is not by their unexplained vote that the bishop will determine on a course of action, but on the reasons they have adduced for it. I believe that, where this system works, it works well.

Of course, a bishop never acts in isolation because there is another bond, another relationship, to be considered and that is the relationship with the Universal Church. This is called 'ecclesial communion' and its most obvious expression is in the bond the individual bishop has with the pope, the Bishop of Rome, the successor of the Apostle Peter.

In answer to Peter's profession of faith, 'You are the Christ, the Son of the Living God,' Jesus replied, 'You are Peter and upon this rock I will build my Church . . . to thee I will give the keys of the Kingdom of Heaven' (Matt 16: 18–19). It is sometimes asked if it is on this profession of faith or on the man who made it that the Church is built. This is a false question because, on reflection, one recognises that faith does not exist in an abstract manner, though it might find, and has found, formal expression in credal statements. Rather, it is found in the relationship between the one who professes faith and the object of that faith – in this instance, Jesus as the revelation of God. Indeed, the whole structure of the Church depends upon such dynamic relationships. After using the image of a building in describing the Church, St Paul suddenly asks: 'Didn't you realise that you were God's temple and that the Spirit of God was living among you?' (1 Cor. 3: 16).

The prayer in the Missal for the dedication of a Church reads:

God our Father, from living stones, your chosen people, you built an eternal temple to your glory. Increase the spiritual gifts you have given to your Church, so that your faithful people may continue to grow into the new and eternal Jerusalem.

There is a happy allusion here to the vision of John in the Apocalypse:

In the spirit he [the angel] took me to the top of an enormous high mountain and showed me Jerusalem, the Holy City, coming down from God out of heaven . . . the city walls stood on twelve foundation stones, each one of which bore the name of one of the twelve Apostles of the Lamb (Apoc. 21: 10, 14).

Of course, the reality is much more concrete. We gather round a table whether to plan or to celebrate the Eucharist. Our bonds are expressed in terms of human affection and we hear one another speaking. And so it is that I sit at a round table in the boardroom of the curial office today and see twelve chairs, ten of which are filled, there being two absent on holiday. I have, of course, met all these priests before, on at least one occasion, and some I am in daily contact with. However, round that table we are brothers and our concern is to ensure that we do right by the people of God.

No doubt there will be other occasions on which the subject of our discussions will be more overtly spiritual, perhaps focusing on the sacraments, religious education or the pastoral care of our youth. On this occasion, our focus is on those structures that will enable the continuation of an exchange of reflection and opinion, part of the necessary process of decision-making on matters of policy in the diocese.

After setting the scene, we examine, in turn, the four main items on our agenda. First is the proposed reduction in the seventeen deaneries in the archdiocese, in order to increase their individual importance and reflect the total diocesan social composition. Among the criteria being considered for the shaping of these deanery areas is the desirability of having a social mix, so that those parishes that are well off, in terms of finance and other resources, will be able to help the poorer ones. Another concern is to ensure that there will be sufficient priests to offer the essential services of the Church in the various parishes, as well as those specialist services provided by chaplaincies to hospitals and schools.

We look at the all-important functions of deans – or, as they are called in Canon Law, 'vicars forane' – and this prompts the question, 'What does "forane" mean?' I believe it refers to areas beyond the city which, in this instance, would hardly apply since most of the archdiocese is urban. And, while we like the word 'vicar' because of what it implies – namely, that those who are so appointed take the place of the archbishop and exercise their pastoral oversight with his authority – we think that we had better stick to the title 'dean' as it is more familiar and there is less likelihood that its holders will be confused with the ordained ministers of another Church!

My thought is that, if the deans can fulfil all the functions described as theirs in the Code of Canon Law, I as archbishop would need to look no further for that essential support that I need in fulfilling my office of pastoral oversight and administration in an area which, though geographically quite small, is nonetheless very populous. We decide quickly enough both on the principle and on the number of deans that we would require – namely, nine.

The next thing is to look at the constitution of the Council of Priests. It is agreed, without the need for any additional committee work, that the deans will constitute, *ex officio*, membership of the Council, which will, in addition, have 'around half' of its members 'freely elected' by the priests themselves in accordance with the statutes. With nine deans, the vicar general, the Chancellor and the Director of Pastoral Planning, the Council will number some twenty-five in total.

Discussion of the third item on the agenda, the role of the Chapter of Canons, is enlivened by anecdote since, in an affectionate and not demeaning manner, the younger clergy now see the Chapter as a club of elderly clerics. This is because, up until now, those who have been appointed to it have continued to be members even after their retirement from priestly service at seventy-five.

Today, most people live a lot longer than they used to so it is not difficult to see that, unless some alterations are made in terms of appointment to the Chapter, we will never have anything other than the current imbalance in terms of age.

We agree that it would be good to preserve a characteristic of the Chapter which brings together its administrative and liturgical functions so that not only do we address our pastoral and administrative concerns among ourselves but we bring them before the Lord. Our aim is to seek, in the liturgy, not only the grace of wisdom and the courage to implement what wisdom dictates but ever to give thanks to God for the continued resourcefulness of the Church springing from His grace. How we are to do this will only become clearer when I have had the opportunity to discuss the matter with the Chapter of Canons itself.

The last item on the agenda – perhaps the most interesting and difficult – is to reshape the deaneries by allocating the parishes differently. It strikes me that each of the nine proposed pastoral areas is, in fact, larger than the two smallest of our Scottish dioceses – namely, Argyll with the Isles and Aberdeen! Once again I am aware of the disparity between what I had been used to and the new situation.

Mgr Peter Smith has done an excellent job in taking the map and colouring in the proposed new deaneries, showing that it would be possible to get a certain evenness in size and a fair approximation to what is desirable in terms of social mix. This is not entirely attainable in the eastern extremities of the archdiocese, nor on its southern flank where an earlier rearrangement of parishes to form a new deanery prompted the view that there should be no further change here.

I am coming to realise that it is not only in places like Johannesburg that, within short distances, people live in very different social conditions. Even given the contrast in living standards between areas such as Drumchapel and Bearsden, there is, mercifully, nothing in Glasgow to equal the poverty seen in the district of Alexander in Johannesburg – images of which are on our television screens these days on account of the World Summit on Global Development which is taking place there. Last night I saw a TV news item that followed the Prime Minister as he looked across a bridge at housing conditions there that are an insult to human dignity and which, in so much of the world, are the common lot of the poor. By coincidence, a report on this appears in the press today and I am comforted to see that remarks I have made with regard to poverty in Glasgow have been welcomed by the leader of the City Council and the First Minister has also responded to them in a positive way.

Such thoughts flash through my head as we try to achieve the best social mix we can in the new deaneries. It is clear to us that further thought has to be given to the new ecclesiastical map of the city. It is, therefore, decided that we invite, prior to our November meeting, the comments of parish priests, in light of which we will draft a plan for submission to the clergy.

Wednesday, 11 September

Like most people, I can remember exactly where I was and what I was doing when the fateful events of last 11 September began to unfold. I was at Toledo in Spain when a friend called and alerted me, urging me to find the nearest TV set.

'Something awful has happened,' I was told.

I found a set and watched with horror as the attacks mounted and the death toll spiralled.

Though many miles away and though shocked to the core by what I had seen, my anguish could have been nothing compared to that of relatives of loved ones involved in that awful carnage. Similarly, my sense of disbelief cannot compare to the sheer panic that gripped those responsible for guiding the US administration during those critical hours.

SEPTEMBER

As the days and weeks passed, the question was asked as to whether one's faith had been affected by what happened on that day. I can honestly say that those awful events did not shake my faith, but they did shake my hope. Of course I retained hope that God in his power and mercy could bring good out of such desperate evil. But I found the human hope, which had been so much a feature of our entry into the new millennium, collapsed along with those symbols of humanity's progress that were the Twin Towers.

Crossing the threshold of the third millennium had been such a hope-filled step. One dared to think that, perhaps, nations, peoples and cultures might find a way of co-existing in justice and harmony. Alas, 11 September is the day that will always be remembered as the anniversary of a deadly attack on that hope.

Monday, 16 September

I travel by train from Birmingham, where I've been visiting my sister, to London to meet the Prime Minister. I had received a warm letter of congratulations from him at the time of my appointment and, since my reply, occasional contact has been made with his office with a view to our meeting.

The first opportunity to do so came with his visit, along with Cherie, to open the new St Andrew's Secondary School in Carntyne in June. I took it that his coming was both an endorsement of Glasgow City Council's co-operation in the government-supported PPP (Public Private Partnership) scheme and a sign of his personal support for faith schools.

St Andrew's is located in one of Glasgow's most deprived areas, though you would not think it once you enter the new glass portals of the school, such is the air of welcome and so many are the signs of achievement. The head teacher, Bruce Malone, and his excellent staff deserve the accolade of a visit from the PM.

That event had all the trappings of a royal visit, with a saturation of police officers and a cavalcade of cars with police escorts. There had been a tangible air of excitement when the couple arrived. The limousine sped up to stop outside the school doors, a troupe of pupils accompanied the head teacher in greeting them and I was invited to join the party as the Prime Minister and Cherie were taken on a tour. Mr Blair was in buoyant, even playful mood, perhaps relieved to be away from the stress of press conferences such as he had held that morning in London. He exchanged frequent glances and occasional touches with his wife and they appeared to take pleasure in one another's successful handling of the classroom and games-hall encounters with the young people.

It had been suggested that a few minutes could be set aside for a private encounter but the opportunity did not materialise so here I am in London to meet the Prime Minister on his home patch instead!

The plan is to go first to Dover House in Whitehall, the splendid office of the Secretary of State. Here Helen Liddell, the Secretary of State for Scotland, greets me warmly and with all the skill of a seasoned politician introduces me to a group of visiting Italian government officials who are a little mystified but undoubtedly impressed to find a tame archbishop in the *Palazzo della Onorevole Ministro di Stato per la Scozia*! I am shown around the house, with its handsome balconies overlooking Horseguards Parade and the garden of 10 Downing Street, a narrow walled enclosure with the swings, climbing frames and other playthings of a young family clearly visible.

We walk round the corner to the Prime Minister's official residence, Mrs Liddell showing her pass and explaining my identity and purpose. Inside the famous door of number 10 is a small reception area, from which a long narrow corridor leads to an elegant stair, the walls of which are ornamented with photographs of former incumbents. We go up these stairs and wait in a large holding bay before being ushered into the Prime Minister's office.

I am immediately struck by the Prime Minister's affability and informality. Jacketless, he ushers me to a table and easy chairs in one corner, and someone enters with a china cup of tea while he continues to drink out of a mug.

I am nervous and make a bit of a mess explaining that I have a letter from the Catholic Education Commission asking the government to make sure that, as a result of new European legislation, the local authority – as employer – and the Church – as approval agency in the appointment of teachers in Catholic schools – will not be liable to a charge of discrimination in appointing only or mainly Catholic teachers. He says that government lawyers will look again at that matter but that it is his understanding that this would not arise as a problem. I feel sure that his public support of faith schools will make him doubly sympathetic to our concern. Only by being able to appoint teachers who will share and support the religious and cultural ethos of such schools can we ensure that such schools fulfill their mission.

We have hardly finished this little bit of preparatory business when the PM jumps to his feet, saying, 'I think we're going to have a small disturbance.' I imagine a PA or other courier bringing an urgent message of disaster here or war there or perhaps the untimely arrival of a foreign emissary, maybe even the Lord Chancellor. Instead, Mr Blair pops out for a brief chat with one of his children before returning to take up where we left off.

It is refreshing to see how the great affairs of the day can be laid aside for a short interval while the Prime Minister reverts to his 'other job' – that of being a good father. It is clear to me that his children really are his pride and joy.

Our conversation is now easy. It takes a child to break any tension: '. . . and a little child shall lead them' – Isaiah's words come to mind (Isaiah 11: 6).

For half an hour our conversation ranges over a number of issues, from financial support for hospices, to inner-city deprivation and the prospect of war with Iraq. I sense that the PM's assessment of the American president goes deeper than the Texan skin. He does not demur when I venture that his influence seems to be key to ensuring that the might of America is not precipitously unleashed and that the role of the UN should be a crucial factor. However, I am not Jeremy Paxman nor even a provincial reporter. I am not there to ask questions nor to give answers. I do, however, hand the

PM a copy of a statement, agreed by the Scottish Catholic bishops a few days before, which I believe is balanced in its call for caution while recognising the seriousness of the threat which Saddam Hussein poses. From the beginning, I have thought that only a serious threat of intervention will force Saddam to accept the will of the United Nations. Sabre-rattling seems to be the necessary concomitant of diplomatic entreaty if he is to pay any attention to the latter.

After a while, I feel that I should let Mr Blair get back to his desk. He shows no hurry but courteously accompanies me to the famous black door by which I entered. By happy chance, I meet an Aberdeen MP on my way out – Ann Begg, valiant in her wheelchair. She seems as pleased to see me as I am to see her and I give her a peck on the cheek. I brag that I have just have tea with the Prime Minister! A few paces on, outside the security gates, I am amazed to see a student of the Scots College in Rome, with some American friends. It is quite a coincidence for this Scottish student to spot his archbishop – especially so far from home – and this time it is his turn to brag!

Thursday, 26 September

I'm on my way to Inverness for the final act of my silver jubilee celebrations in the Diocese of Aberdeen. I have as a travelling companion the parish priest of St Margaret's, Lerwick, Fr Gerry Livingstone, who has been to Glasgow to visit his mother. He is Glasgow-born but has, through his deceased father, a connection with the north of Scotland. His father was born in Brora. It is this connection that has led him to the Diocese of Aberdeen as a candidate for the priesthood.

He tells me that Shetland has had the best summer 'since the war' – day after day of sunshine. At first people put a finger to their lips in case mentioning several days of good weather in succession might break the spell. In fact, before the summer was over his expectation was of days of warm sunshine, little wind and summer clothes being de rigueur.

My own memories of pastoral visits to Shetland confirm that the weather there can be extraordinarily fine. I used to tease the parishioners that tales of bad weather were purely fictional, so fortunate was I during the times of my visits – though I do recall finding it difficult to stand up against the wind at Sumburgh Airport. There was one famous occasion when, with Archbishop Maurice Couve de Murville, the Archbishop of Birmingham, I was stranded for several days during an August visit. My companion was delighted at the enforced delay which, after a couple of days, we decided nonetheless to bring to an end by taking the P & O ferry to Aberdeen instead.

The sea was like a millpond and it was only as we approached Aberdeen Harbour that we came out of the sea haar to see the place bathed in bright sunshine. He remarked, 'What pride an Aberdonian must have on approaching his city from the sea.'

Aberdeen's harbour takes the visitor almost into the centre of the city. The skyline at this point is dramatic, Marischal College Tower, the Scots baronial towers of the Salvation Army Citadel and the Townhouse all vying with one another for attention at the Castle Gate. Then there are the spires of the city's central churches – including that of what was once Scotland's largest parish church, St Nicholas', and the elegant spire of St Mary's Catholic Cathedral, the highest in the city, of which I used to be so proud.

Unfortunately, this magnificent skyline has been spoiled by obtrusive high-rise buildings, the worst offender being St Nicholas' House, the office of the city council built within yards of the tower of the Townhouse and the magnificent tower of Marischal College. One can console oneself with the thought that, some day, better town planning and a greater sensitivity to a city's profile will see the offices demolished.

But back to the journey to Inverness. I'm driving there myself with Fr Gerry Livingstone as my passenger and, unfortunately, the day is rather dull though it is dry. Already the Scottish countryside is beginning to take on autumnal colours and reveal another of its seasonal garbs. I have a pang of nostalgia, just like I experienced a few weeks ago, when I took the road to Stirling. The rugged and majestic Highlands lie ahead, fringed with the rich farmlands of the north-east of Scotland. It is interesting to observe how consistently the east coast carries this fringe of good pasture land, in some places, very broad but, in others – for example, in eastern Sutherland – it is reduced to a mere strip of ground.

We sometimes think of the Highlands and Lowlands as describing lands to the north and lands to the south. But really the Highlands proper are to the centre, west and north-west of the country, with the Lowlands spreading up from Berwickshire, broadening out in what we now think of as the industrial belt, through Fife, the Mearns, Aberdeenshire, along the Moray coast into the Black Isle and Easter Ross and up to Caithness.

Our route takes us to Stirling, where the castle continues to fascinate the traveller by its majestic silhouette. Wallace's Tower stands proud against a backdrop of hills which begin to provide the main feature as we come to Perth, that elegant and beautifully situated city on the Tay, built, as so many other cities have been, where travellers could cross a river. In this case, going towards the north-east or the north-west – the latter being our direction through the hills of Perthshire by Pitlochry and Blair Atholl, with its magnificent white castle of the Dukes of Atholl. Then we continue through the creases in the hills, now more barren, until we reach Kingussie and Aviemore, once popular and now regaining something of their popularity as tourist places.

We stop at Aviemore to see St Aidan's Catholic Church, perched on a hill and surrounded by trees. The last priest had cut an opening in this arboreal fence and, in conjunction with the other ministers in town, erected a large cross to mark the Great Jubilee of the year 2000. Its elegant black shape, seen against the backdrop of the Grampians, is enhanced by the framing of the trees.

Aviemore is looking attractive, with flowers in baskets hanging from every lamppost and gardens beautifully laid out. Certainly every attempt is being made to seduce the visitor into staying. We, however, resist the temptation and proceed to Inverness.

SEPTEMBER

How magnificent the view is as you come over the hill and suddenly have, in front of you, the broad panorama of the Beauly and the Moray Firths, of the Black Isle and the hills of Sutherland to the north-west, with land stretching as far as the eye can see towards the horizon. The base of this beautiful view is the new city of Inverness, the ancient 'capital of the Highlands', now fulfilling, more credibly, its title and role as the administrative centre for the Highland Region. The spindly bridge in the middle-distance carrying the main road from the north, the A9, underlines the city's role as a communications and shopping centre for the whole of the Highlands. Indeed, geographically, this is the largest administrative area in the British Isles.

We arrive at Mgr McDonald's busy presbytery in the early afternoon. There is a warm welcome for his erstwhile bishop and his erstwhile curate.

Friday, 27 September

My jubilee mass tonight at Inverness is, as I could have confidently predicted, a happy event, with representatives from many parishes in the deanery. Also represented is the most northerly parish in Shetland in the person of its parish priest, Fr Gerry Livingstone, my companion on the journey north. A family from Orkney also made the trip, as did the parish priests of the mainland parishes, including Fr John Allen from my former parish of Wick and Thurso.

I decide to use the first reading of the day set in the Lectionary. It seems to be particularly apt, being a famous passage from one of the so-called 'wisdom books' of the Old Testament, Ecclesiastes. My sermon reflects my mood, looking back fondly on days gone by.

> According to the author of Ecclesiastes, there is a time to be born and a time to die; there is a time for everything, says the preacher.
>
> The time has come for me to pack up my memories of twenty-five years as Bishop in the Diocese of Aberdeen and go where

the Lord has sent me. It is time to reflect, with thanksgiving, on the graces of all those years and a time for regretting my failures. Perhaps it is a time of waiting for the seeds which have been sown to come to fruition – the harvest lies head. Jesus himself used the parable of the sower and hinted at the patience needed for the word of God to produce its fruit.

What he applied to the field, he also applied to the individual as a single grain of wheat: 'I tell you, most solemnly, unless a wheat grain falls on the ground and dies, it remains only a single grain; but if it dies, it yields a rich harvest' (John 12: 24).

The preacher in Ecclesiastes asks:

What does a man gain for the efforts that he makes? I contemplate the tasks that God gives mankind to labour at. All that he does is apt for its time; but though he has permitted man to consider time in its wholeness, man cannot comprehend the work of God from beginning to end. (Eccles. 3: 10–11)

Indeed, one has to see one's own efforts as part of a coordinated plan extending over time, a series of seasons succeeding one another bringing their own climate, as it were – at times inhibiting growth, at times increasing it.

St Paul uses that image in his First Letter to the Corinthians:

After all, what is Apollos and what is Paul? They are servants that brought the faith to you. Even the different ways in which they brought it were assigned to them by the Lord. I did the planting, Apollos did the watering, but God made things grow. Neither the planter nor the waterer matters; only God, who makes things grow . . . We are fellow workers with God; you are God's farm, God's building. (1 Cor. 3: 3–7, 9)

When I was ordained bishop twenty-five years ago, I used the words of St Gregory the Great in which he asked that he might 'see life whole'. I am not yet on the final ridge but I can see enough to be able to thank God for all the things he has made grow over these twenty-five years.

It is time, therefore, for thanksgiving and I am deeply grateful to you all for giving me that opportunity. Your affection and support over the years have formed part of the fabric of my life, your efforts intertwining with mine to create the fabric that we now hang up to view, as it were.

I was privileged to be appointed in a parish where, physically speaking, the church at Thurso was two years old and I have lived to help celebrate its silver jubilee. I had the satisfaction of seeing to the re-ordering of St Joachim's, Wick, and the rehabilitation and alteration of the adjoining property for the benefit of the parish. I had the privilege of laying the foundation stone and blessing the new church at Tain, having earlier presided at the blessing of the new church at Alness. It was in my time as bishop that the former bakery at Ullapool was acquired and transformed into the lovely church that exists today. I have seen extensive works, undertaken both by Canon Stone and Mgr Robert McDonald here at Inverness, and rejoiced at the beauty of what has been achieved. Looking over to the Black Isle, I was happily instrumental in acquiring the former drill hall at Fortrose, which now serves as our church and is a delight to parishioners and visitors alike. Looking across to real islands – namely, to Orkney and Shetland – I was able as bishop to ensure the reorienting of our lovely little church in Kirkwall and the rehabilitation of the house. The present work on the presbytery at Shetland was initiated during the latter months of my time as bishop and I hope that the Lord will allow me some time to see the results.

It was a sadness to see the closure of Fort Augustus Abbey, though there has been this compensation in that the former lodge has been turned into a presbytery and chapel – the intimacy of the latter contrasting markedly with the magnificence of the former abbey church but not being without pastoral benefit.

I restrict my memories to those of the Highland deanery,

which has, of course, its own character, its own history, its own hardships, in terms of the Catholic faith, and its own hopes for the future, some of which I have had the great grace of seeing unfold.

St Paul used another image of growth, that of building: 'By the grace God gave me, I succeeded as an architect and laid the foundations, on which someone else is doing the building. Everyone doing the building must work carefully' (1 Cor. 3: 10).

And so my thought is that, if we can see an upbuilding of the Church in the physical sense, we can be certain that there has been spiritual growth. The sacraments of the Church guarantee that and I can think back with great satisfaction on all the masses, at which I was privileged to preside, and the many hundreds of confirmations that I administered over the years up and down this lovely land.

St Paul continues in his Letter to the Corinthians by applying further the image of a physical building:

For the foundation, nobody can lay any other than the one which has already been laid, that is Jesus Christ. On this foundation you can build in gold, silver and jewels, or in wood, grass and straw, but, whatever the material, the work of each builder is going to be clearly revealed when the day comes . . . Didn't you realise that you were God's temple and that the Spirit of God was living among you? (ibid.: 10–13, 16–17)

Whereas our first reading was the reading set for today in the Lectionary of the Church, I chose this passage from St Luke in order to remind myself and you that we have to be ready at all times to do the Lord's work, whether it be to sow, to wait patiently or to reap or – to change the image – to wait as faithful servants on the Lord's will: 'See that you are dressed for action and have your lamps lit. Be like men waiting for their master to return from the wedding feast, ready to open the door as soon as he comes and knocks' (Luke 12: 35–6). Whereas this passage is frequently used to comfort those who have witnessed an unexpected call from the Lord, my thought at present is not so much of that but of the actual wait, which sometimes seems long – as long as watches in the night – but issues always in the light of day, that day which dawns the brightness of Christ.

Let us keep one another in our prayers as we share the watch and await the day.

As I look around and see people I had first known more than twenty-five years before – in some cases forty years earlier – I cannot but reflect on the passing of time and the changes it makes even to our physical appearances and comportment. I think, sadly, that, perhaps in some instances, this might be the last time I will see some of these dear faces, though I readily promise to be back if excuses can be found for such a visit.

Over a hundred people attend a dinner in my honour at the Columba Hotel on the banks of the Ness. This is a delightful affair during which I am presented with a beautiful painting of the Moray and Beauly Firths, executed by an artist of the St Mary's congregation. I then receive a quite exceptional tribute in the form of a book, a Festschrift, assembled in my honour by a group of contributors under the editorship of the director of the Ogilvie Institute, Mr – now Deacon – Tony Schmitz. He explains the formation, gives thanks to the contributors and describes the contents. Mgr Robert McDonald gives an elegant little speech and I speak extemporaneously, saying how I deeply appreciate not only the gifts, but all the affection and goodwill that lie behind them and to which they will always be a constant witness.

Saturday, 28 September

Before returning to Glasgow, I decide to revisit Pluscarden. I have heard that the abbot, a contributor to the Festschrift and I believe the author of its idea, is ill and so expect to find him in bed. But, when at last my presence is observed and I am brought into the abbey proper, I discover that he is dressed and ready to come down. In fact, despite a back complaint that has been causing him considerable discomfort, he has managed to journey to Rome and has just returned. It is a joy to see him. I join the community for lunch.

However, it is the hour or so of my unobserved prayer in the Abbey Church – where the medieval squint enables you to see the Blessed Sacrament in the adjacent Lady Chapel – that is the greatest pleasure of the visit. My thoughts naturally go back to the days before the monks had returned when, then a boy, I would be taken on occasion with my mother and sister in my father's car to picnic in the cloister. We dreamed then of the monks' return and today that dream is a reality, much appreciated in Moray and beyond.

October

Thursday, 3 October

I am on my way once more to Rome for a variety of reasons and causes which my diary will uncover. The first is to attend, as comoderator, the executive of the Joint Working Group – a follow-up to the plenary in Sweden in May.

Sunday, 6 October

Today the Holy Father canonises Josemaria Escriv, a Spanish priest who died in 1975. Best known for founding the organisation Opus Dei – the prelature which promotes the ideal of holiness in every day life – his rapid rise to the glory of the altars has provoked controversy among some observers and has been warmly welcomed by others. Since I have been in Rome for the last few days, I accept the invitation to attend.

I leave the Scots College in what I think will be plenty of time, accompanied by the vice-rector, Fr Paul Milarvie. Alas for us, our every path seems to be blocked and every attempted shortcut turns out to offer nothing more than further delay. Eventually poor Fr Paul drops me some way from St Peter's Square, in the vicinity of which around 400,000 people had gathered.

Dressed as I am in the black soutane and purple sash of a bishop, my path is somewhat eased and I find myself being ushered on to the *sagrato*, or stepped area, in front of the Basilica just as the Holy Father arrives. As I take my place, one of the members of the Vatican Security Forces quips: 'You had better hurry or the mass will not be valid!'

From where I sit I am able to take in the vast array of the faithful, gathered not only in the piazza itself but all down the great Via della Conciliazione, the processional avenue of Mussolini's creation leading up to St Peter's. And still further they reach, as far back as Castel S. Angelo and the banks of the Tiber.

Later I discover that some had found themselves unable to secure even such a remote vantage point and had to make do with sound-only participation in the mass from the neighbouring streets around Borgo Pio.

The Holy Father pronounces the formula of canonisation at 10.23 a.m. Though there is no doubting the joy of the crowd, expressions of exuberance are few, such is the recollection of this extraordinary congregation. I feel privileged to be one of the 400 bishops, archbishops and cardinals present near the Holy Father at this moment.

How deeply moving it is to see so many gathered in respectful prayer in that great amphitheatre of faith, to celebrate the goodness of a man of our time, a man whose message that 'sanctity is for everyone' is so essential today. In the words of Cardinal José Saraiva Martins, Prefect of the Congregation for the Cause of the Saints:

> By canonising the founder of Opus Dei, the Holy Father offers all Christians a real model. Adding him to the rank of the saints, the Supreme Pontiff proclaims him a part of the treasure of the Church, of the patrimony of sanctity that constitutes her and of the sap that nourishes her. The new saint belongs to all Christians, as much an intercessor for their needs as a model of inspiration for their lives.

Following the ceremony, I am whisked off to a reception in the magnificent Palazzo Taverna. My table guests are none other than the editor of the *Catholic Herald*, William Oddie, and his wife, with whom I shared some good-hearted banter over one of his pet subjects, liturgy.

Monday, 7 October

The visit to Barga and the Garfagnana region starts unpromisingly enough. For one thing the rain comes down and dogs our visit, though the journey north from Rome is pleasant enough weather-wise and also fleeting, as all motorway journeys tend to be.

We – Ronnie Convery, my Director of Communications, and I – leave the Scots College after lunch. He is driving a hire car and we are soon on the Raccordo Anulare, the great ring road round the Eternal City, and then on the *autostrada* making our way north in the direction of Florence. We wend our way in and out of Umbria and Tuscany, perhaps the loveliest regions of Italy, but I must confess to some bias since my grandparents came from the northern parts of the latter region and we are on our way there now.

Ronnie is not, strictly speaking, on holiday since I have invited him along with a view to our doing some work together both en route and at our destination. The fact that he is a fluent Italian-speaker, however, has played a part in my reasoning and, as we speed north, it seems a good opportunity to engage in a conversation in Italian to help my own fluency. Despite my Italian blood, I have never fully mastered the language.

Looking back, I regret first of all that what little my parents had of the language was not passed on to my sister and me. Secondly, and perhaps less justifiably, I regret that linguistic fluency had not been seen by the rector and staff of the Scots College, during my time as a student there, as an accomplishment to be encouraged. Indeed, everything conspired against our learning Italian since our lectures were in Latin, the space between lectures were restricted and there was little opportunity for us to make use of the language. And, during the times when we could have used it – namely, when shopping – speaking became unnecessary owing to the prevalence, even then, of supermarkets which required little skill on the part of foreign shoppers. In any case, we even had to obtain permission to go shopping as it was regarded as an unnecessary preoccupation. We went, by rule, to the Gregorian University in company; on afternoon walks in company; and on holidays in company. I believe we were even supposed to speak Latin going to and from 'the Greg', although by my time that was a forlorn hope.

Ronnie and I decide to split the journey to Barga and stay overnight in Lucca, partly because we have had enough travelling for one day and partly because it seems a good idea for me to show Ronnie something of the beauty of that less known Italian city. We arrive, apparently by chance, at the very gate at which the local tourist board has its prestigious presence in what appeared to be a gate to an earlier circle of walls. Lucca, after all, is one of the most walled-in towns in Italy, with a series of walls marking the gradual expansion of the city from Roman times onwards.

I had promised Ronnie that it would be an easy matter in October to find a couple of rooms in a suitable hotel here. I am proved wrong and, after half an hour's effort on the part of the tourist board, we come out with a slip of paper promising us two rooms in two different houses in an old part of the city.

The young woman who has been helping us is efficient, despite appearing to be dying of a cold, and she scribbles directions on a map and sends us on our way. These directions prove to be anything but clear and, if we need any experience of driving in the narrow streets of a city that is closed to most traffic most of the time, we get it in Lucca! Backwards and forwards we go, time and time again, in danger of going down one-way streets the wrong way, turning the map this way and that, stopping for directions, but eventually reaching our destination. The rooms prove to be simple, comfortable and clean, though not what we had originally anticipated.

We are staying near the amphitheatre, a delight to the visitor who loves history and architecture. And since it is built on the site of a Roman arena, its houses, although of differing heights, are held together by both a string course, running throughout the square, and a harmony of colour. We could have a meal outside, in the square, but decide otherwise and find a restaurant nearby. And, so fortified, we retire for the night.

Tuesday, 8 October
It is to the cathedral that we wend our way this morning, again finding Lucca a challenge to our sense of direction. We pass other churches on the way, built in the twelfth and thirteenth centuries

in a Romanesque style particular to Lucca and its environs. Unfortunately, however, the cathedral is not to be seen at its best, since it is undergoing restoration, but we find a mass in progress and are duly uplifted spiritually. We also pay a courtesy visit to Matteo Civitali's *'Tempietto'* – the 'Little Temple' – which houses the famous statue, *'Volto Santo'* of Lucca – the 'Holy Face'.

There is a tremendous downpour. An opportunistic salesman provides us – at a price – with an umbrella and then, fortified by coffee from an elegant coffee shop on the way, we collect the car and we're off once more in the direction of Barga.

It's an interesting phenomenon that the many Italians, who came across to Scotland at the end of the nineteenth century and for many decades of the twentieth, originated mainly in three distinct areas of Italy. Those in Edinburgh came from an area south of Rome and north of Naples near Cassino, Picinisco. Those in the north-east of Scotland came, in large part, from the region of Parma, in particular Borgo Val di Taro. But those who settled in Glasgow and the west of Scotland came from Barga and the Garfagnana region. Indeed, it was from the latter area that three of my grandparents arrived, during their early adulthood, in Scotland and England. The remaining grandparent, my maternal grandmother, came from over the Apuane Alps, which run north-west to south-east along the Versilian coast, from a place called Chiavari. My parents were, in fact, second cousins, a further illustration perhaps of what must seem already evident – namely, that the pioneers brought over their *compaesani* to work for them.

I have been to Barga many times over the years – the first when I was a student at the junior seminary at Blairs. I was a recently-turned sixteen-year-old and I was, by very generous dispensation, allowed to go with my mother and sister (my father already being dead) for Easter in Rome in the Holy Year 1950. We stayed on that occasion with some friends with whom my father and mother had stayed on an earlier visit. They had been there both for the Holy Year 1925 – the year of their marriage – and again in 1933 when I was already *in utero*. Indeed, my mother claimed that I was a Holy

Year baby! – since I was born when the 1933 Holy Year had been extended, in order to mark the 1900th anniversary of the death and resurrection of Christ, to include Easter of 1934. I had been a much-wanted child but my parents had had to wait nine years after their marriage for my birth. It had been a sort of novena in the Catholic sense – namely, a period, multiplied by nine, during which one prays for a special intention. Since so many nuns, not least those at the Convent of Mercy in Elgin, were engaged in an enterprise of prayer, I have often claimed to be the answer to maidens' prayers!

In 1950, Europe was being reconstructed and I can recall the last stones being laid in the Via della Conciliazione, today a broad avenue leading up to St Peter's Square. It was an image of post-war peace-making. From Rome, we visited our relatives in Barga. At that time, we still owned our paternal grandparents' home, little more than an empty shell, and a farm at a lower level in the valley of the Serchio river. Hilaire Belloc, author of *The Path to Rome*, once traversed this. He remembered it as a 'baking oven' and described Fosciandora di Garfagnana as sounding like a clash of cymbals.

The first things to catch Ronnie's eye, as we arrive at the city walls at the Fosso, are the flags, fluttering in the wind – the Italian tricolour, the Union Jack and the Saltire. I remember someone telling me that they were going to put out the flags for my coming and it looks as though the reports were true! In fact, these flags have been there since the earlier visit of the Lord Provost of Glasgow, Alex Mosson, whom, at one time, I had hoped to accompany. He had a double purpose in visiting Barga this summer. The first was the connection this place has with so many of the citizens of Glasgow. The second was his desire to open an exhibition of paintings by John Bellany who, in recent years, has made his home for at least part of the year in a former farmhouse, very close, in fact, to where my great-grandparents once lived.

If I had entertained any hope of visiting Barga quietly or even of entering it unobserved, any such hope is immediately dispelled.

As soon as I get out of the car I recognise a woman who has spent many years in Scotland and who is a friend of friends. On hailing her, Elda Pieri comes over at once, full of excitement – an excitement evidently shared by her Yorkshire terrier. I naturally enquire about her sister, Clara Piacentini, who is an occasional telephone correspondent, advising me of her comings and goings to and from Italy and keeping an eye on my relatives in Barga when I am nowhere near them.

There had to be the usual photograph taken, 'to send home to Clara'. Alas for the poor dog, however – it nearly meets its end. Deciding that it should not appear in the photo, Elda fixes its lead to a high gate post and this leaves the dog hanging by the neck! Thankfully the terrier survived the excitement – and its near hanging!

We are, by now, within yards of my cousin Agostino Caproni's shop. Described as an *alimentari*, it is a shop selling the best of Italian food and wine and, I suppose, it is what we would call a delicatessen. The warmth of the greeting is something I know to expect but I'm sure Ronnie is somewhat overwhelmed to find himself immediately embraced as a member of the family.

The third person I set eyes upon – who comes over and positions herself where I cannot fail to see her – is the sister of a former parishioner at Wick. And so it continues during all three days of our stay in Barga. Old friends, old family and new family – being an archbishop does wonders for people's historical memory and becomes an irresistible motive for the discovery of family ties. I eventually come away with a photo of my father at ten months and that of a great uncle Daniele, brother of my paternal grandmother, whose great nephew was discovering in truth a relationship with someone he had never met before but whom he imagined, because of the name, might be a *parente* – the all-encompassing word to describe a relation at any level of kinship.

We are staying in one of the three hotels in Barga, the Alpino – this one being in some senses a rival to my cousin's hotel, the Libano, but without any offence being taken. It is closer, Agostino admits and, therefore, more convenient for keeping in touch with us, which proves to be the case. Indeed, two of the attractions of my cousin's hotel – namely, the garden and the view – would have been superfluous anyway because it hardly stops raining during the course of the three days. Scottish weather for the Scots visitors. It seems to be some sort of ironic tribute!

This evening we have one of the many meals which mark our three days in Barga but this one is special since it brings together the closest members of the family. It is an occasion to recall memories of days long past and of people, including my mother, now long departed from us. These are the inevitabilities of the occasional coming-together of families separated by time and space.

Wednesday, 9 October

This first full day is largely spent in a car for what the Italians call a *gita* – a pleasant day out. Agostino is the driver and our other travelling companion is Mgr Piero Giannini, the parish priest of Barga for almost as many years as I have been a bishop. He is now an old friend and, in fact, surprised me by arriving in Glasgow for my installation as archbishop in February.

Inevitably, our journey is through the Garfagnana region, the deep valley of the Serchio river which has hill towns on either side like medieval fortresses defending the high ground. Sadly, the terraced slopes of these villages are no longer cultivated as vineyards, though their stepped shape makes them look like ziggurats. The higher slopes are planted with chestnut trees. These sweet chestnuts provide flour for polenta – a staple food of the area. I'm told that bags of these chestnuts were taken to Britain by returning emigrants, providing them with the opportunity of making some money by roasting and selling them during the winter months in the city streets. Of course, this particular form of catering was not suitable for the summer and was replaced by ice cream. From such an unlikely beginning, came the proliferation of cafés and restaurants that are so much associated with the Italian community the length and breadth of the country.

My family once had a farm near here. Despite my grandmother forbidding it, my grandfather had acquired it along with another relative to whom he had lent the money to allow him to pay his half-share. This money had been brought from Britain with strict instructions from my grandmother that it was to go straight into the bank. My mother always maintained that there was a curse on that farm because everything happened to it. An earthquake destroyed the house, a war destroyed the fields, hail killed the cattle and any number of excuses were given for its failure to produce anything more than enough profit to allow my mother to buy herself a two-piece suit made for her by a seamstress in Barga. How she loved that suit!

Apparently, my grandmother did not speak to my grandfather for a whole week on his return to Britain. Ironically, though, after the Second World War, when all the money my grandparents had placed in bank accounts against their eventual return to Italy had lost its value, only this poor farm proved, on sale, to have had any value at all.

There was, however, my grandmother's house at Treppignana, which I never pass now without a pang of nostalgia. It's difficult to describe the emotion of seeing a Scots name over the bell push. Like so many other houses in the area it has now become the holiday home of northern visitors. Indeed, our first call was to Maria Vittoria Ricci, the wife of our former *fattore* (farm manager), Luigi Ricci, who was the man responsible for ensuring that the income from the farm was divided, according to Tuscan law, with 51 per cent going to the owner and 49 per cent to the *contadino* – a concept that is notoriously difficult to convey in English and which is probably best described as a person who works land they don't own. (Of course, the *contadino* always, in a sense, had a better deal since he could call upon the actual food produced on the farm for his sustenance.)

We are warmly welcomed by Maria, now well into her eighties. Luigi, who is on the verge of his nineties, still cultivates the Tuscan soil as he has done all his life. Maria urges us to go out and find him in the fields on the land he loves. But Mgr Piero and Ronnie decide that this family duty does not include them and so, leaving them behind, Maria and I go in search of her husband, only to find him coming towards us with his arms outstretched in greeting. It is an emotional reunion. News is exchanged – he tells me of his hospital visit and his remarkable return to reasonable health – memories of the past are recalled, including the time he took me on his motorbike to see the 'Volto Santo' of Lucca when I was a student. In those days, before safety helmets and speed limits, I recall hanging on with all my strength, praying fervently that I would survive Luigi's driving long enough to appreciate the visit!

I am to meet up with Ronnie and Mgr Piero in Riana, the neighbouring village from which my grandfather came. There is no sign of them anywhere. The village seems deserted. I assume that a pious monsignor is to be found in the village church but not a bit of it. At this moment, they are in a cantina, tasting the wine. Their 'excuse' is that, while walking through the tiny, steep streets, they stopped to examine the great barrels in which, for centuries, wine has been stored in this region. Their interest has apparently been amply rewarded. The *contadino* whose barrels they were examining apparently insisted that they join him to sample this year's vintage. After suitably positive expressions of appreciation, the *contadino*'s wife was summoned to find a bottle of last year's wine so that the visitors could offer an educated comparison. The poor monsignor, who is a near teetotaller, protested in vain before submitting to the ordeal and offering his definitive judgement on which *vendemmia* (grape harvest) had been better!

Close by is the converted farmhouse now belonging to John Bellany. I had heard much about him but had not expected to meet him, certainly not so soon nor so warmly. He and his wife, Helen, are standing on the stairs leading to the first-floor entrance at the side of their house when we drive in.

It is as warm a welcome as we received from my Italian relatives. Really, the place is having its full effect on two people who have fallen in love with this part of Italy and have decided to make their home here. In through their studio we go, passing paintings stacked one in front of another – these have been returned not so long before from the exhibition which Alex Mosson had opened in Barga. We go downstairs for coffee, out through French windows to the terrace and the garden and along to the limonaio, formerly a greenhouse where lemons were grown and now beautifully converted into a conservatory. They have found paradise here, they say, and I can believe it – even in the rain!

In truth, the purpose of this visit is to ensure that a painting, that is to be presented to me tomorrow, as a surprise, is to my taste. John explains that if I do not like it he will not be offended and will supply something more to my liking. So, when he says he has 'something for me', I assume that this is the painting in question. However, now that he has discovered that I was born in the north-east, he has decided to give me a painting of a north-east fishing boat instead of the view of Barga which he had planned. I am delighted at its rich colouring and find it hard to put into words my gratitude for so excellent a gift. Only then does it transpire that this is something *extra* – a personal gift on our first encounter. What he then revels is the 'official' painting – the one I am to receive the next day at the official reception.

It makes an immediate impact. It is the face of Christ on the cross. I cannot help but recall the 'Volto Santo' of Lucca and it proves to be something of a leitmotiv for the following twenty-four hours.

'Yes,' say John and Helen, 'we'd love to come to dinner tomorrow at the Ciocco, an elegant country club high above Barga, but can we come beforehand to the mass at the Duomo?' I was, of course, delighted.

Thursday, 10 October
Today is the formal *accoglienza*, the welcome, given to the son of *emigrati* who has not only 'made good' but seems, in the eyes of the people, to have 'made very good' by becoming an archbishop!

It starts like this. We are collected by cousin Agostino and taken

175

to the Barga city gates. At this point, Ronnie provides me with the text of my speech, in Italian, on which we had been working. But, as it is in his handwriting, I am working through it, familiarising myself with the words. When the car stops, I look up to find a crowd of dignitaries standing there at the city gates, ready to receive me in some style.

I emerge from the car, notes and pen in hand, to be greeted by the mayor or *sindaco*, Professor Umberto Sereni, a professor of modern history at far-away Udine University and director of the local newspaper, *Giornale di Barga*, which was founded by his father. He introduces me to rows of officials, among whom are marshals and colonels of the *Carabinieri* and the *Guardia di Finanza*, coming from as far away as the provincial capital of Lucca and immaculately dressed in those stylish uniforms which we have come to expect from Italy's forces of law and order. By now I seem to be as much a guest of the whole province of Lucca as of the city of Barga, such is the influence of Barga's *sindaco*!

Together we make our way in some sort of procession through the narrow streets of the old town. I am disconcerted to see in almost every shop window a picture of myself in full liturgical dress, with captions announcing my arrival and the events that will mark it. I suggest that even the dogs will be frightened by such a picture – and it is true that I had not seen on earlier visits such tamed animals. On reflection, it is perhaps the sight of the marshals and colonels, rather than the presence of an archbishop, that has had this pacifying effect on Barga's canine population!

The formal welcome takes place in the main room of the *Palazzo Pancrazi*, the town hall. It is already partly full of people awaiting our arrival. If his speech of welcome is typical of the style of presentation used by the professor to his students in Udine, then I can imagine they are fully engaged and much entertained in their studies! As good professors do, he produces his evidence – in this case of the links between Glasgow and Barga over the years. He has in his hand a letter dating back a hundred years addressed to a distinguished Italian patriot, Senator Antonio Mordini. He was a close collaborator of Giuseppe Garibaldi in the work of Italian unification – his statue stands proudly below the great cedar of Lebanon in front of the hotel owned by my cousins.

The letter tells of how Italians in Glasgow at the end of the nineteenth century have been somewhat ashamed by the misdeeds of one of their number – in fact, the man in question has had a death sentence hanging over him. But the letter goes on to reveal the determination of the small Glasgow Italian community to stick together, in order to win some respect from the host community, and asks Senator Mordini to become a patron of a self-help charity which they have established there.

The mayor draws from this document all sorts of lessons: the community spirit of Italians abroad; the close historical ties between Glasgow and Barga; and the tradition of cordiality which has characterised relations between Italian immigrants and native Scots over the years. I sense, as he continues, that I am being asked to assume something of a leadership role in order to bring together the Italian community in Scotland. And this feeling is confirmed later when we visit the editorial office of his newspaper. There Professor Sereni frankly admitts that he hopes I will become a *'punto di riferimento'* or a focus for Italians abroad. Of course, today Italians living in Scotland are not in need of the same sort of protection that might have been required a hundred years or so ago. Then they were among some of the newest stones in the building of a city that became great on the shoulders of its immigrants.

After this energetic speech, I reply in more subdued terms, though my words seems to strike a chord with those present. I illustrated the many *legami* or links which I have with Barga and its environs, not only by ties of blood but by bonds established through my pastoral ministry in the north of Scotland. Members of the Cabrelli and Cardosi families whom I served as parish priest in the fourteen years I had in that northerly outpost of the Diocese of Aberdeen that is Wick and Thurso are now back in Barga. I inevitably have to make some reference to the gift that I anticipate but which has not yet been presented to me. For most people there, I imagine the sight of the painting which John Bellany presents to me is their first glimpse of what, in a moment of inspiration, I call the 'Volto Santo di Barga' – the Holy Face of Barga.

It is to this theme that I return when, during the solemn pontifical mass in the Duomo later that day, I give, as expected, a short address. Seeing John and Helen in the congregation, I decide that it would be a good idea to deliver my homily not only in Italian but also in English, for I want them and others to know that a gift of such imagination and quality is one I deeply appreciate.

By happy coincidence the first reading of the mass of the day is taken from St Paul's letter to the Galatians. In the extract read, St Paul reminds them that they are foolish if they do not recognise that salvation comes not from the law but from the cross of Christ. I spoke of the two 'Holy Faces' of our trip – the first in Lucca cathedral, the famous 'Volto Santo' of that town, and the second, the painting I received this morning, John Bellany's modern rendering of that same suffering face of Christ. I speak of that face of Christ which expresses not condemnation or anger but, rather mercy and compassion. I develop the sermon to speak of the humanity of Christ which He shares with us and which allows Him to feel genuine compassion and solidarity with us.

As the mass draws to a close Mgr Giannini, after expressing in tender terms his long friendship with me, presents me with an image of the crucified Christ. This time it is based on the famous painting associated with St Francis of Assisi before which he heard the words of Christ asking him to 'build up my Church'.

Among the members of the ladies' choir who sing so beautifully during the liturgy, I am happy to notice two members of the family – Agostino's wife, Anna Maria, and his daughter, Federica.

The final act of today is the dinner to which John and Helen have been invited, along with other friends of Agostino, including the ever-present *sindaco*, whose effusive commentary on my sermon proves almost to be a repeat performance. Never before have I had a sermon analysed in such detail – at least publicly! It is a delightfully memorable meal in gracious surroundings – a hotel just below the place where my grandparents had their humble abode and above the valley where, the day before, we stopped to be photographed by the signpost indicating the Via dei Conti. It seems that all that has gone before has led here.

Friday, 11 October

Leaving is as emotional as arriving. Eventually we get on our way, returning to Rome via Pisa, not in order to see the Leaning Tower – though, indeed, we do – but to pay a courtesy visit on the archbishop through whose territory I have been stomping about, though with some excuse, over the previous days. We find Archbishop Plotti, warm-hearted and welcoming, in a large palazzo which certainly doesn't have quite the same character as himself but which he somehow fills with his presence. He seems to know about all that has gone on and so there is no need to make excuses or to ask for absolution! He is clearly delighted that a son of the Diocese of Pisa has returned to his roots.

I recall, years before, feeling a tremendous sense of obligation to my past when I celebrated mass in the presence of the Archbishop of Lucca in the cathedral of the 'Volto Santo'. The occasion was the day of the *emigrati* – the day set aside to salute those Italians who had left their native land to build a new life abroad. It was celebrated as part of the 1200th anniversary of the 'finding' of the Holy Face of Lucca.

Archbishop Plotti explains that Barga, while being geographically in the middle of the Diocese of Lucca, is an enclave of Pisa due to the fact that, for many years, it had been an outpost of the Duchy of Tuscany. This latter administration could not abide the thought of its fief being under the spiritual direction of the neighbouring republic of Lucca!

The archbishop entertains us to lunch and then calls one of the superintendents of the cathedral to come and fetch us so that we might have a guided tour of that great building and its baptistery.

So, culturally fortified and culturally laden with paintings and books, we take the path to Rome again – not like Belloc, wearily on foot but swiftly via the *autostrada*.

Saturday, 12 October

Today I find myself – as the Italians would say – at a small table among others hugging the corner of a building, the façade of which faces the Palazzo Farnese, short by the hotel where I have gone to join a group of knights and dames of the Holy Sepulchre in Rome for a holiday. For the first time in many days, I am alone and enjoying the opportunity to look around and reflect. In the immediate foreground is a bottle of unstated provenance but which, by my taste, comes from the Castelli Romani. It accompanies a plate of *fettuccini ai funghi*. Being a Tuscan by blood, I love my mushrooms!

I intended to have only one dish but the enchantment of the surroundings and the contentment of being on my own for a little conspire to persuade me otherwise. So, when the attentive waiter asks me what I would like for my next course, I decide, upon the very mention of it, to have *saltimbocca alla Romana* – a delicious dish of veal and parma ham sautéed in white wine with sage. The literal translation is 'jump in the mouth roman style' and it lives up to its name beautifully!

How pleasant it is to sit here observing but being unobserved; waiting for the warm October sun to turn the corner and flood the table; hearing voices in many languages from adjacent tables and from the street beyond the flower pots, over which the rather raucous voice of the one I take to be the *padrone* rises as effort-lessly as that of an operatic tenor against the counterpoint of a supporting chorus. I muse that perhaps you might find an experience like this elsewhere. But perhaps not if you look be-yond the foreground to catch a glimpse of a fountain constantly playing in a basin of Egyptian granite which once adorned the hall of the Baths of Caracalla, more recently famous for opera than for bathing, so my guidebook assures me. How useful to have one at hand, particularly when awaiting the arrival of *saltimbocca*.

What I see beyond I already know – a palace built by Sangallo for Alessandro Farnese who became Pope in 1534 under the name of Paul III. This was another family with a son who 'made good' who needed to establish their presence in the city with a building of commensurate dignity – and the Farnese were among the most successful in so doing. I can see the upper windows between the *ombrellini* (sunshades) and, unobstructed above them, is the great cornice which Michelangelo designed for the building, magnificently overhanging the walls and crowning the structure in a way too often forgotten by modern architects who leave us with unadorned boxes. At a certain point – another Italian phrase – I feel as if I am on the first rung of a ladder called ecstasy!

My idyll is ended when the waiter approached with my bill. For some reason he addresses me as '*dottore*' – a form of address which was also used by the signora at the desk to which I am directed to pay. I am, I should explain, '*in borghese*', as we used to describe a mode of dress which somewhat concealed our clerical status.

Whatever the reason the waiter may have, I suppose I have some justification in being called 'doctor' since the University of Aberdeen gave me a doctorate some years ago '*honoris causa*'. However, on my first holiday thereafter I thought to assume the title of 'doctor' and thereby minimise, as far as possible, the fuss occasioned by my episcopal status. In other words, I wanted to go incognito. Alas, this somewhat backfired when a small group of us, five at the most and including a priest friend, gathered round a table at the invitation of the tourist guide at Luxor, part of ancient Thebes of Upper Egypt. Believing that it would be our intention to be 'matey', the guide suggested that we introduce ourselves.

'In what branch of medicine do you specialise?' she asked, to the evident interest of the rest of the party. The thought that at least one of the women could be pregnant or someone else might have Egyptian tummy terrified me but, since I did not wish to blow my cover, I answered rather pompously, 'When on holiday I prefer not to say . . .'

I thought there was pity in the eyes of my colleague since my embarrassment must have been all too obvious. I did eventually disclose to our Egyptian guide, a professor from the University of Cairo, that I was a bishop when I asked her to take me and my companion to a service at the Coptic Cathedral where I knew there was an opportunity to meet the Coptic bishop. He sat at the end of a long corridor following the sacred synaxis and greeted people benevolently, giving sweets to the children, counsel to the troubled and a blessing to all. I believe that my loss of anonymity was a fair price to pay for the opportunity of meeting a prelate of the ancient Coptic Church and greeting him as a brother in Christ. Ecumenical instinct had prevailed. (By that time I also thought that Egyptian tummies and unforeseen pregnancies were no longer a threat and the interest of fellow British travellers unlikely to detain me in matters spiritual!)

However, I have never again attempted to use the title of doctor and so the waiter's use of it in addressing me is curiously well aimed. He deserves his tip! I leave and, while passing by the Theatre of Marcellus, a lorry driver calls to me, without provocation, as I walk in front of him, *'Viva la bella Roma!'* – 'Long live beautiful Rome!' Truly, the city seduces both native and visitor.

Sunday, 13 October

While you cannot live without beauty, the delight of Rome must give way to more pragmatic considerations when we must choose where best to educate our future priests. It is not long before the question arises again: with little more than thirty students for all the Scottish dioceses, which of our seminaries – Rome, Salamanca or Scotus in Glasgow – should be sacrificed, even temporarily?

The Scots College in Rome is the oldest and arguably the most prestigious of our colleges, though Salamanca follows close behind, both in historic foundation and in the opportunity it provides for able students to graduate in philosophy and theology at a distinguished university. It could be argued for Scotus, however, that it is in a direct line from Aquhorties (1799–1829) and Scalan

(1715–1799), though I do not recall at the opening of Scotus any mention being made of its ancient antecedents.

Scalan was as important as any foreign college in providing the priests needed by the remnant Catholic community to ensure its survival. The home seminaries of the twentieth century – Partickhill, Bearsden, Cardross, Newlands, Drygrange, Chesters, Gillis and Scotus – have all served in the education of priests for the Scottish mission. The advantage of these home seminaries, particularly in more recent years, is that they provide practical pastoral experience during the years of a priest's training. Indeed, it may seem surprising to the casual observer to know that students used to return from Rome and Spain without any such experience, gaining it in their first appointments as curates or assistant priests. I did this, myself, at St Mary's Cathedral in Aberdeen – as curate to Canon Lewis McWilliam for three years and I continued there for a further three years as curate to Fr James Robson.

At present, students from our colleges abroad are given opportunities for pastoral experience during their long vacations and I don't think anyone would deny that this need is ever more clamant. With a reduced number of students, it is possible to conceive of it being given to all of them under a single programme which can also spill over into the months of their formal academic training as has increasingly been the case in recent years both in Italy and in Spain. Indeed, with the greater fluency of students in the languages of the countries in which they live and the universities they attend, there is something to be gained in their being able to help out in local parishes and schools.

There are, however, three other areas of formation: the academic, the spiritual and the human – the latter embracing personal and cultural development. Rome and Spain provide, in that order, the broadest opportunities for the study of those academic subjects in philosophy and theology, essential to a priest's education – Rome having the advantage of a number of universities, including at least one which teaches in English. Spiritual formation, on the other hand, can be done in any circumstances where there is sufficient input from experienced spiritual directors and the same might be said, making the necessary adjustments, for the human development of students.

Perhaps one of the most important elements in this latter field is living in community. I have always thought that, no matter what other reasons may be given for differences in the style of preparation of priests, the experience of living in community provides, in practice and on reflection, an education in human relationships. Assuming the orthodox faith of candidates and a sufficient level of intellectual ability, there is nothing more important, in my book, than student priests having and developing interpersonal skills – a style of personal engagement with others which is easy, friendly and encouraging. More important than the inevitable financial considerations, therefore, is the need to ensure that our colleges are healthy communities comprising sufficient numbers of candidates to stimulate and test students in their capacity to live with and serve others. Those who argue that, because so many priests live on their own, a so-called 'monastic' preparation is unsuited to their training, have missed the point. A priest may live on his own, but he lives among people, serves people and must, as a good pastor, be in daily contact with them.

All these thoughts come to mind as I sit on the terrace of the Scots College today, musing on the experience of the previous days in Rome. I am alone since the rector, staff and students have crossed the busy Via Cassia to take part in the celebrations for the local parish's patron saint. These were marked, of course, by mass but also by a gathering, thereafter, of parishioners for a barbecue, fireworks and goodness knows what else. Such events give a practical example of the way in which a college abroad can engage its students in pastoral and social encounters and probably, in so doing, give practical expression of the universality of the Church to a group of local parishioners.

I have often thought of our college in Rome as something of a Scottish cultural embassy in one of the great centres of civilisation.

OCTOBER

Sunday, 27 October

For the first time, in the absence of Mgr Peter, I find my way cautiously to a Glasgow parish with a street map in hand. I am at St Jude's, Barlanark.

Being an archbishop does not significantly alter the problem of anonymity when you seek a respite from duty, though I have noticed already that I'm better known in Glasgow than I ever was in Aberdeen. Or perhaps Glaswegians are just more likely than the reserved Aberdonians to show that they recognise someone and approach them. It also seems a peculiarly Glaswegian practice to gather signatures of those whom they think are important. Autograph hunting of a sort. It starts, I have discovered, with children but Auntie Betties and Mammie's Mammies provide the excuse for a requested autograph on the part of those who have, at least in other respects, left childhood behind.

But don't get me wrong. It's good to feel wanted and a signature, such a small token, can give pleasure. And being last in the queue for the buffet seems a reasonable price to pay for the pleasure given. However, be assured – and I speak from experience – that there is never a lack of food when parish ladies have provided for after-mass refreshments, even after the street urchins of the Missionaries of Charity have alighted upon it!

But enough's enough of rambling, as of food.

November

Saturday, 2 November

Tonight I am able to make my first formal visit to the University of Glasgow on the occasion of a mass in the university's Memorial Chapel for All Souls Day. In recent days, I have learned that I am the first serving Archbishop of Glasgow to offer mass here since the Reformation. My predecessor had been due to preside at a mass to mark the university's 550th anniversary in June 2001 but had died a week before it took place.

I was warmly welcomed by both the university's Church of Scotland chaplain, Rev Stuart McQuarrie, and its Catholic chaplain, Fr John Keenan.

At the start of the mass, I made reference to its historical significance, referring to the Reformation as 'unfortunate events several hundred years ago . . .'. I believe the congregation readily understood my allusion!

The mass is embellished by the magnificent singing of the university choir, who perform Fauré's *Requiem*. How wonderful it is to hear the music perform in its 'natural setting', not as a concert piece but as an expression of the faith of the Christian in eternal life and as an plea for God's merciful judgement on those who have gone before us: *'Dona eis requiem'*.

My sermon focuses on the central mysteries of life and death, as this seemed appropriate given the occasion. I mention the mystery of individual human freedom, a matter of faith to the Christian – a freedom which in no way determines the action of God nor hinders the fulfilment of His plans. I note:

It is the classical conundrum of the relationship of human freedom to divine omniscience and omnipotence which has exercised philosophers down through the centuries and, no doubt, puzzled generations of undergraduates in corners of this very institution over the last 550 years!'

And I add:

The underlying mystery is our own creatureliness, the contingency of our own being on which fragile base is, nonetheless, built that relationship with God by which we are not only called to be but, in truth, are, children of God.

I quote from the Holy Father's letter to the university on its 550th anniversary when he recalled its role in society and the Church's desire to be a partner in the quest for truth.

In our own day the Church continues to regard the university with esteem and respect, seeing academic research and teaching as vital and essential components of the formation of the whole human person. The Church, with its witness to the transcendent realities of life, sees in the university a collaborator in the quest for truth, justice and knowledge.

Finally, I seek to sum up the mood of reflection and remembrance in these words.

This evening we recall with piety the founders of this institution. Those who planted it in a thoroughly Christian soil, offering it as a motto, the words by which Christ described himself and, in a sense, by participation, every work related to him, '*Via, Veritas et Vita*' – 'the Way, the Truth and the Life.

We recall in piety those outstanding men and women who have served the University of Glasgow as teachers, researchers and companions in pursuit of wisdom over the centuries and those many thousands of students who, exercising that humility which is a necessary pre-requisite for true knowledge, have studied here, gathering its riches, among which there has never been missing the pearl of great price.

After the mass, I am one of 150 guests of the Catholic chaplaincy, the Friends of Turnbull Hall, together with representatives of the Senate and Court of the University. Lord Gill, the Lord Justice Clerk and a proud alumnus of Glasgow University and its Catholic chaplaincy, offered a witty welcome and Professor Frank Pignatelli proposed a toast, once more sprinkled with humour. The latter recalls the somewhat impish sense of humour of my predecessor who, on the occasion of his being given the cardinal's red hat in 1994, presented Professor Pignatelli and his wife to the Holy Father.

'This is Frank Pignatelli, Your Holiness,' Cardinal Winning said, before adding with a twinkle in his eye, 'You will remember that your predecessor Innocent XII was also a Pignatelli . . . '

To which piece of useless information the Holy Father was heard to reply, 'Eh, beh . . .', which Frank loosely translated as 'So what!'

All in all, it is a most enjoyable evening at which I am heartened by the genuine affection and wishes of support on the part of many.

Sunday, 17 November

The village of Croy, near Cumbernauld, has the distinction of being almost 100 per cent Catholic. Irish miners settled in the village and built a handsome church and presbytery on the crest of the hill. I first heard of this village during my days at Blairs College – now I'm on my way to celebrate its centenary as a parish.

As we approach the village I have a sense that Mgr Peter is uncertain as to where we should be going. He pulls into a lay-by and points ahead. There, approaching me, all smiles, is the young parish priest, Fr Paul Friel, one of my first appointments.

Suddenly I am aware that, close by, is a uniformed silver band. This is the famous Croy Silver Band – no bishop or archbishop, I learn later, has ever visited the parish without being drummed into it! A procession is formed and I am led up the hill into the extensive and beautifully kept church grounds – no signs of graffiti or vandalism here! A clutch of priests is waiting for me in the sacristy, including former parish priests and the young Mgr Hugh Bradley – a son of the parish – who gained the title of Monsignor for his several years of service in the Congregation for Catholic Education in Rome. Croy's influence extends thus far – as wide as its unique reputation and that of its band!

We have a glorious celebration!

Thursday, 21 November

The day I have been looking forward with great expectation – and just a hint of apprehension – has arrived. This is my first meeting with all the priests of the archdiocese. I arrive at the Thistle Hotel in Cambridge Street – everywhere I look, I see clergy.

A well-kent face connected with Rangers Football Club – so I am told, being innocent in such matters! – emerges from the bar, rubs his eyes in disbelief at seeing quite so many priests in one room and quickly retreats.

Before long the large room, set up for the meeting, is filled to capacity – some 200 priests are present. In a corner Paul McSherry is taking snapshots of each of them so that we have a full photographic record of the priests of the Archdiocese.

I am impressed at the technology which Fr Paul Conroy and Fr Paul Murray have put in place. Mgr Peter calls us to order. Mgr John Gilmartin, as vicar general, introduces me and we're off!

Here is my address:

Those of you who, throughout the years, have experienced change from one parish to another will guess at the upheaval in my life as I moved from Aberdeen to Glasgow earlier this year.

Aberdeen is my native diocese and I hope I will be forgiven if occasionally I refer to it as if it were still mine. In a sense it still is since I was born in it, educated in it and became a priest of it

in 1958 – although my actual ordination was in Rome in the final
year of my studies as a member of the Scots College. I think all
of that is known from my potted biography in the Catholic
Directory.

What I have lost, above all, in my move to Glasgow, is the
company and friendship of the priests of the diocese and the
many parishioners throughout the whole of that vast area, whom
I came to know over the years, and the members of religious
orders, both male and female, whose hospitality I have enjoyed
over the years.

In compensation, however, I am truly blessed with six times as
many priests in Glasgow and, as yet, an unknown number of
religious brothers and sisters and, of course, many, many more
diocesans.

I cannot tell you how much I have valued our conversations
and how impressed I have been at your courtesy, your frankness
and your remarkable dedication to the people whom you have
been appointed to serve. I cannot imagine any bishop in this
country or elsewhere being able to boast as I can boast of you
after the interviews I have had over these recent months. What
you have shown me and which was intended, of course, was my
need of you and, can I say it without creating a false impression,
your need of me? A bishop without his priests is useless; a body
of priests, without the linking and leading of their own shepherd,
can lack direction or feel unsupported in their endeavours. I am
certainly now one of your own and I want to be available to you
whenever you need me.

While Glasgow and Glaswegians were not unknown to me, I
did expect a cultural change but I think the cultural difference
has been greater than I had anticipated. Aberdeen is a small
diocese in terms of population but vast territorially. Of course,
cultural differences are not simply to do with locality – though a
rural diocese has got a different feel to an urban one.

However, it is in the origin of the people that perhaps the
greatest difference is noted. The Church survived in the north-

east to an extent unknown in Glasgow. If we accept that, in the latter part of the eighteenth century, there was little more than a handful of Catholics in Glasgow and the surrounding area, then the Church here is composed in the main of two immigrant communities that, for some time, were in conflict – though that is a story I do not need to tell today. One came from within Scotland, drawn to the industrial belt from the poorer areas of the Highlands; the other from across the Irish Sea, cousins indeed to the Scots and once, in medieval times, sharing the same name – 'Scoti'.

We see new waves of immigrants today, both political and economic refugees, such as many of our forebears were. We need to give them a warm welcome since we ourselves have found a home in this land or city.

It is to be expected, and in no way to be regarded as something untoward, that the Church in Glasgow should be aware of the ethnic and cultural origins of its people and be comfortable in celebrating them. On the other hand, we are now part of the history of Scotland and our Scottishness should not be worn lightly as if it were simply an outer garment. We are part of a Church that was one of the chief influences in the shaping of Scotland. For a thousand years, until the Reformation, Scotland knew no other church than the Catholic Church. Some of its most ancient surviving buildings are its cathedrals and abbeys. Its most ancient Institutions are those of the three universities founded by Papal Bull. Some of its oldest schools were the song schools attached to the cathedrals. What survives of its Renaissance music was that of the Chapel Royal and collegiate churches. Little survives of its art and furnishings but we know that the churches were rich in them, as the late medieval statue of Our Lady of Good Success – or, as it is also known, Our Lady of Aberdeen – which is now in a Brussels church, evidences.

Exactly one thousand years elapsed between the death of St Mungo and the death of the last Catholic Archbishop of Glasgow in the mediaeval hierarchy, James Beaton, who died in Paris in

1603. This coming year, we will celebrate the 1400th anniversary of the death of St Mungo and I mean to make it an opportunity for celebration, for thanksgiving, for being reminded of our roots and for ecumenical endeavour. I am not likely to forget that Glasgow's motto is 'Let Glasgow flourish by the preaching of the Word and the praising of His name'. I am suggesting that the archdiocesan coat of arms, which the Lord Lyon King of Arms is presently considering, should bear the motto, *'Predicatione Verbi'*. The proposal for the shield is a set of silver keys on a blue background or perhaps gold keys on a green shield – the colours and the design of the former hinting at the Saltire of Saint Andrew, the patron of our cathedral church, the latter to Glasgow as the dear green place. The crossed keys of course allude to the keys of the kingdom and the symbol of the Papacy, of the Roman Church, of which the Archdiocese is proud to be the *Specialis Filia*.

When our St Andrew's Cathedral was opened in 1816, it was said to be the largest and finest Catholic church in these islands. Its builder was one of those priests from the north-east in whose footsteps I have, to some extent, come – Alexander Scott. Our cathedral, though it is modest in size, must nevertheless be dear to us. Planted on the very banks of the Clyde, it welcomed the boatloads of immigrants from across the Irish Sea, whose courage in the face of adversity and whose fidelity in a religiously alien land have so greatly enriched the Catholic Church in Scotland. We will have to do something soon to correct some structural defects in the building, to rebuild the organ and to redecorate the walls. I venture to suggest that it might be the time to look more imaginatively at what we might do, for it is a church which calls for some expansion in order to provide a suitable liturgical space for the clergy of the diocese. A cathedral should reflect the pastoral importance in the life of the Local Church as clearly as it expresses itself as the seat of its chief shepherd. There has been a number of somewhat intimate meetings between diocesan officers and architects, who are well-known in the city and whose services we have engaged in the past, to look to the way in which, if circumstances, financial and otherwise, were favourable to us, we could develop the cathedral site.

Earlier this year the Scottish Catholic Historical Association noted the centenary of the death of Charles Eyre, the first Catholic Archbishop of Glasgow in the restored hierarchy of Scotland. He is a man to which the Catholic Church in Glasgow owes so much. It mounted a very successful seminar to mark the anniversary. Distinguished historians painted a clear and engaging picture of the development of the modern Archdiocese, illustrating how effectively and generously it had responded to the needs of its poor, whether for the basic necessities of life or for education. The Archdiocese, with its sponsorship of thirty-four social work projects, its Pastoral Care Trust, its support of the Catholic School system and its dedication through its many religious communities to the spiritual and corporal works of mercy, continues in that proud tradition of service and I hope I will be equal to the task of maintaining it.

Before moving from the historical perspective, I think we should note the three hundred years between the death of Archbishop Beaton and that of Archbishop Eyre. It would be useless to pretend to any more than a notional continuity of the great medieval church with the Church of the Restored Hierarchy. Of course, those years were not without Catholics noted for their deeds of valour, the greatest of which is perhaps the martyrdom of St John Ogilvie at Glasgow Cross in 1615. There were Catholics in the crowd then and there were Catholics in the city and its environs over the years, their spiritual needs being addressed by stout-hearted priests trained and ordained abroad or in home seminaries, the most notable of which was Scalan. I would love our children in Glasgow to know more about those men and those times. However, the point I want to make is that, during those years, the Gospel continued to be preached – if not in communion with the Apostolic See, nevertheless, with some sense of continuity with the past. It is something we should acknowledge. In the increasing friendships we have, as a Church, with other Churches and Ecclesial Communities in Glasgow, we can share our love of our respective historical communities, as we engage, ever more closely, together in the work of proclaiming the Gospel in our secular world – the field in which we are to broadcast the seeds of faith. I hope that the Year of St Mungo will provide such an opportunity. Already we have had, through the agency of Glasgow Churches Together, an opportunity to share our ideas with the Moderator of the Presbytery of Glasgow, whom I have known for years, the Episcopal Bishop and other Church leaders and we have met enthusiasm with enthusiasm. I have already invited the next Moderator of the General Assembly of the Church of Scotland, a Professor from Aberdeen University and of a distinguished Church of Scotland family, Professor Iain Torrance, to visit us here in Glasgow and to preach in St Andrew's Cathedral. I believe I owe it to him that I am an Honorary Professor of Theology of Aberdeen University!

I have spoken of the cultural differences between the Church or diocese I have left and the Church or Archdiocese to which I have come. Different histories give us a different outlook. Even when people are living in close proximity to each other, it is possible for some of them to feel just as isolated as those separated by physical distance. This has come home powerfully to me in the discussions I have had with you. How many times you have mentioned people's fear of coming out at night, of a sense of intimidation and of their subjection to vandalism and vulgarity of many sorts. If we add accounts that have been obtained more scientifically to the anecdotal evidence – statistics on violence, sectarian strife, as well as on poor health, drug addiction and alcoholism – we have the darker side of a picture wherein we see, in greater relief, the sturdy devotion of so many faithful members of the Church and the tenacity of their piety. Many areas of the city are areas of social deprivation. The greatest deprivations of all are the cultural and the spiritual which result, undoubtedly in part, from endemic poverty but which must also be related to the loss of the sense of community values, with the loss of faith or of its practice. That I know I have to face along with you.

In this first introductory session I have tried to tell you where I have come from and where I am in my understanding of the Church, its history and its present situation.

I have mentioned, in passing, our ecumenical commitment; I have set up a Review Group to take stock of the present situation and to see how we can continue to expand our relationships with the Church of Scotland and the other Churches and Ecclesial Communities in the city. This committee is chaired by Sister Maire Gallagher, SND, who, until recently, was the representative of the Catholic Church on the Central Council of Action of Churches Together in Scotland and Convenor of the Council. Among other members is Brother Stephen Smyth who is employed part-time as Ecumenical Officer to the Glasgow Churches and, as such, is Secretary of Glasgow Churches Together.

I have also had a meeting under the auspices of Glasgow Churches Together with other church leaders in order to put to them ideas we have had for the celebration of the Year of St Mungo. These ideas were explored in a special meeting I convened at Scotus with members of the Archdiocese I knew to be interested and, in some ways, already engaged in ecumenical relations and in the celebration of the St Mungo Jubilee.

Other meetings will take place shortly, following which I hope to be in a position to give you further information about the year. However, let me say already, at this juncture, that the celebrations will hopefully be as much at parish level as inter-parish or inter-Church. In other words we hope to have a full diary of events, some of which will have been initiated at diocesan level and some your very own, whether purely parochial or in conjunction with neighbouring churches. We also hope to engage our schools, both primary and secondary, in these celebrations. I regard it as a signal blessing that I have, in my first full year of office, such a significant anniversary to celebrate.

DIOCESAN STRUCTURES

We do not have to invent the Church. It has already been given to us – yes, by Christ, in terms of its message, its hierarchical structure, its authority, its sacramental system and its charismatic endowment. It is important to remember this when we talk, as we will later, about pastoral planning. Suffice to say, at this moment, that our pastoral plans must sustain, enhance and make more effective what has already been given to us.

The focus in this section is on the way in which pastoral leadership is provided within the diocese. When I was appointed, my first thought was how I was going to manage, given my age and inexperience of the Glasgow area. I visited Pablo Puente, the apostolic nuncio, with one or two questions before confirming my readiness to accept appointment. I knew that, prior to Cardinal Winning's death, he had requested, in principle, the appointment of a couple of auxiliary bishops. The process of identifying and nominating suitable candidates was well under way when he died. I asked whether I might be given an auxiliary bishop and the nuncio gave me some comfort in believing that, if I requested the Holy See for such an appointment, I would be favourably heard.

Those of you who were among the first in the interviews will recall my asking you the question as to whether there readily came to mind the name of one or more of your peers who might be suitable for nomination. The question was always connected with the question about the advisability of my so proceeding.

Let me be frank. As time went on, there was, on the one hand, a clear lack of agreement as to nominations and, on the other hand, some hesitation as to the necessity of my obtaining an auxiliary.

This is not to suggest that there was any want of respect among priests for a largish number of their peers who were

regarded as exemplary committed priests. Those who wondered
at the need often related it to the Sacrament of Confirmation, of
which the Bishop is said to be the Ordinary Minister. Present
practice within the diocese has, however, shown that another
solution is available – namely, the appointment of delegates to
preside at the Sacrament of Confirmation. You are well aware
that my first administrative act in this area was to indicate that I
would grant a Faculty to all parish priests who applied to act
themselves as my delegates in confirming their parishioners. This
removed some of the urgency in addressing the question of an
auxiliary bishop.

The more I reflected on the matter, asking myself the question,
'What precisely do I need?', the more I began to realise that what
I needed were men who could act for me in a vicarious fashion,
extending pastoral leadership into all areas of the diocese – men
who could advise me about the specific needs of their areas and
of the priests which served them; men who could identify local
resources, in terms of personnel and ecclesiastical plant, and who
were capable of organising their colleagues in addressing such
problems as providing chaplains for hospitals, prisons and
schools; men who could be aware of parishes with special needs
and, of course, of parish priests in need of support of one sort or
another. I thought of the Council of Priests and the way in which
members of that Council should not only be able to represent the
needs of their colleagues but have my confidence in so doing
and, as members of the Council, be able to implement what
might be decided in it or as a result of its deliberations.

For a number of years, as Bishop of Aberdeen, I had begun to
see the value of the role of dean, as it was explicated in the Code
of Canon Law. The dean was once an important person within
the body of the clergy, though I suspect that, over the years, his
position was undermined by some uncertainty as to his essential
tasks and, if we are to speak frankly, by the role being exercised
by senior priests, some of whom, near to retirement, were
perhaps battle weary! Appointing younger men, after

consultation, had resulted in an enhancement of the role and I could see, in particularly successful deans, how valuable their ministry could become both to their fellows and to the bishop.

And so, at a certain point, I decided that, instead of looking towards one or more auxiliary bishops or, indeed, vicars episcopal, I should look again at the role of dean.

I go on to explain how examination of the present deanery structure and proposed amendments came about, before outlining the various changes to the Council of Priests, College of Consultors and Chapter of Canons that I noted in my diary entry for 2 September.

PASTORAL PLANNING AND PLANS

By planning, I mean that activity which comprises reflection, examination and decision-making relative to the implementation of the Church's Mission.

That mission is both *ad intra* and *ad extra*. In other words, our efforts must be directed to ensuring that the faithful are educated in their faith and have a proper appreciation of the Sacraments which they celebrate in the Liturgy of the Church. At the same time, we have to be proclaiming the faith to those outside, whether lapsed or faithless. For those who respond to that proclamation, we need to provide an appropriate catechesis. The Rite of Christian Initiation of Adults and the preparation of children for the reception of the Sacraments both fall within the area of planning. We need to make arrangements to undertake these tasks in an effective manner, wisely seeking the advice and support of one another and co-operating with other agencies such as the Catholic school at both primary and secondary levels.

Pastoral plans are the necessary fruits of such planning. They comprise aims, objectives and methods. The aims, being universal, are likely to be agreed on an archdiocesan basis. It is hardly likely that we would be inventing aims. Rather, it would be a case of prioritising those which are already discernible in the mission which Christ has given us.

The objectives are more particular and address the actual pastoral situation in which we find ourselves. It would be reasonable for us to have a series of diocesan objectives. It would also be reasonable for individual parishes to have specific objectives related to their own specific needs.

Methods are the ways in which we implement our objectives. Some may be well tried methods, such as keeping in contact with parishioners by house visiting, or they may be new in that they are using modern technology not known to an early generation of pastors. I think of ways in which people are increasingly using personal computers and e-mails. Also the ease with which we can now reproduce news-sheets and pamphlets enables us to keep in contact with parishioners by such means.

One method of promoting a sense of community and providing cells of evangelisation is the setting-up and fostering of faith-sharing groups, prayer groups or neighbourhood groups, which are presumably a form of faith-sharing groups but based upon some more detailed planning strategy.

What is important, it seems to me, is that we assess carefully not only what is needed but also what is feasible, given the particular circumstances of the archdiocese and our individual parishes. What may be suitable in one place may not be suitable in another. I think we have to acknowledge the need of flexibility.

Having said that, I think we also need to acknowledge that the Second Vatican Council very clearly established the rights and duties of lay people to be engaged in pastoral planning, since their characteristic vocation is lived out in the world, in the area of family, of business, of work, of social intercourse, and, if properly informed in the faith, their recommendations as well as their support are essential in any pastoral pogramme both within the parish and in the archdiocese itself. It is not only prudent for us to consult the laity and engage them with us in our pastoral endeavours – we have a duty to do so.

The minimum requirement, it seems to me, is that, in every parish, there should be a Pastoral Council – namely, a group of lay people, however chosen, elected or appointed, who will form a stable group within a parish, meeting regularly according to a constitution, which will be drawn up in each parish under the leadership of the parish priest, in conformity with the norms which, in such circumstances and according to Canon Law, the bishop should issue.

I speak frankly when I say I have sensed a certain weariness on the part of many of you – and, in some circumstances, a real frustration in implementing the Pastoral Plan as drawn up and presented to you. It may be that, in some circumstances, the expectations are unrealistic by dint of the nature of the parishes you serve. In other instances, you may have come to a parish where a previous parish priest has not been very successful in undertaking the first steps. Indeed, it may be necessary for us to go back to first principles and ensure that we all understand what we are about and why. Only then can we be sure that, with a sense of ownership of what we are doing, we can tailor what is on offer to our specific needs.

I am also very conscious that, with a decreasing number of priests and consequently an ever-increasing burden of pastoral care, it is very necessary to engage others in assisting us. For this reason, drawing both on my experience and on the consultations that I have had with many of you when the subject has been raised, I propose to you the establishment, in the Archdiocese, of the Permanent Diaconate, open to married men of maturer years who are able to support themselves and their families, undertake the studies required and who can offer good service, over a wide range of talents and opportunities, to the Church.

Furthermore, I would see the importance of establishing means whereby a larger number of lay people might be educated in their faith and for ministry within the Church, ranging from Extraordinary Ministers of Holy Communion to catechists and teachers of the faith to fellow adults.

With regard to this latter, I have already held a meeting with interested persons, both clerical and lay, and I am asking a small group of educational specialists to visit the Maryvale Institute at Old Oscott, Birmingham, which has had increasing success in delivering adult education by the distance learning mode. I am persuaded that this mode can be fruitfully used in a city environment as well as in dispersed dioceses, such as Aberdeen, where we have had a successful engagement with Maryvale through the agency of the St John Ogilvie Institute which I established.

There are other possible components of an adult education programme. In every instance, I would be looking for support from the clergy not only in promoting it but also in their offering their services as tutors and spiritual advisers to those engaged on courses.

I see both of these initiatives extending the Pastoral Plan of the archdiocese into an area of need and, while the number of persons benefiting from such an adult education programme as I have just described may be smaller than the potential for those attending neighbourhood groups, over the longer term, this may well prove to be the more effective means of evangelising both *ad intra* and *ad extra*.

I hope that both these initiatives – namely, the introduction of the Permanent Diaconate and the drawing up of a programme of adult education by distance learning mode – will have your fullest support.

It is not, therefore, a matter of inventing a 'new programme'. The programme already exists – it is the plan found in the Gospel and in the living tradition. It is the same as ever. Ultimately, it has its centre in Christ himself, who is to be known, loved and imitated so that, in Him, we may live the life of the Trinity and, with Him, transform history until its fulfilment in the heavenly Jerusalem. This is a programme which does not change with shifts of times and cultures, even though it takes account of time and culture for the sake of true dialogue and effective communication. This programme, for all times, is our programme for the third millennium.

Now I turn to the archdiocesan programme for the preparation of children for the reception of the Sacraments.

I drew from my interviews the strong impression that there was virtually universal agreement with and support for the situating of the proximate preparation for the Sacraments in the parishes to which the children belonged. When, last year, the bishops were invited to respond to a questionnaire which sought to gauge the degree to which the catechism of the Catholic Church had been received and the degree to which it had become the source of material for local catechetical programmes, the invitation came from the Congregation for the Clergy and not from the Congregation for the Doctrine of the Faith or the Congregation for Catholic Education and Seminaries. This in itself clearly indicated that the function of catechises was under the direction of the clergy, not properly or directly the responsibility of the Catholic school. Catechises means more than religious education. It implies formation and preparation and that is essentially a pastoral task.

In making our response on behalf of the Bishops' Conference of Scotland, the Commission for Christian Doctrine and Unity to which the document had been sent, made the point that, in Scotland, Catholic schools had traditionally involved themselves in the preparation of children for the Sacraments. In other words, Catholic teachers had seen it as part of their task to prepare children for the Sacraments and it is my understanding that, in many parishes, hitherto, priests had relied solely on the school which, at the right season and according to the right age group, would bring children to the local parish church for the celebration of the Sacraments.

While our Catholic teachers deserve to be applauded for this work which may be thought to be beyond the call of duty, the parish clergy, parishioners and parents have a role to play and the policy of the archdiocese, as I have understood it, has sought

202

to provide them with sufficient opportunities for the discharge of these shared responsibilities.

Several things strike me as being important. Firstly, that teachers are not given any impression that what they have done, in the past, has not been appreciated, nor is their help, in the present, not still solicited.

Secondly, that the parish priest is able, along with sufficiently trained parishioners, acting as catechists, to complete, as far as possible at the stage reached by the children, their understanding of the Sacraments they will be receiving and to ensure that they are sufficiently spiritually prepared for their reception.

The engagement of parents is essential since the duty of bringing their children up in the faith and implicitly, therefore, bringing them at appropriate age for the reception of the Sacraments, lies primarily with them. Parish and school need to work closely in order to ensure that this is understood and that the duties which parents have in respect to these matters is discharged. Here we face a problem which is less one of organisation than of the preparedness of the parents to fulfil their duties. I suppose there is a danger that non-practising parents will seek to shove their responsibility on to the school or indeed to put school and parish at variance. There are practical pastoral problems here, sufficient to give most priests headaches, and all I can ask of you is that you do your best according to the principles to ensure that the children of your parish are well prepared for the Sacraments and receive them fruitfully.

Having said that, I am well aware that the underlying concern of many, if not all of you, relates to the fact that many children – perhaps, in some circumstances, even the majority of them – are not themselves practising since they come from non-practising families but these families are, nevertheless, keen to see their children reaching what they presumably regard as grades of achievement. I anticipate that the questions I have been identifying are those which will need further reflection in the light of experience with a view to our revising, if necessary, archdiocesan policy. A great deal is at stake here and I do not claim any particular wisdom to propose answers to the questions. What we must avoid, however, is any lack of courtesy or friendliness to those who contact us, however unreasonable their attitudes may seem at times. We have, at all times, to reflect the *mansuetudo Christi*.

I have in mind all the Sacraments of Initiation, commencing with baptism. I know that already many of you have the practice of inviting parents to come and learn something of the responsibilities that they are undertaking when requesting the baptism of their children. Such encounters are not only important for the imparting of information but also for gently leading parents back into an appreciation of their faith and the need of prayer in their lives.

I know that the postponement of First Communion until Primary Four age has been widely welcomed, not only in this diocese but also elsewhere in the country.

I come now to the difficult matter of the age for the presentation of children for confirmation. You know that there is no unanimity among the bishops with regards to this matter – just as I know that there is no unanimity among you with regard to the age of children's confirmation.

Let me place at least some of my cards on the table. For me, the question is a pastoral one not a liturgical one. For me, the tradition is what we have received and not the going back to some golden age in the past. For me, the model is what is appropriate for children and not a reflection of the pattern of adult reception into the Church. Reference is sometimes made to the Rite of Christian Initiation of Children but my interpretation of the instructions there is simply to remind ourselves that children who have reached the use of reason cannot be treated as if they had not. In other words, they must go through a process of understanding of their faith before their baptism and the reception of the other Sacraments of Initiation.

Reference is also made to the practice of the Orthodox

Churches. Their practice will always be of interest to sacramental theologians but it does not govern the practice of the Western Church. That practice has developed, it seems to me, with a richer understanding of one of the essential aspects of the Sacrament of confirmation and that is its missionary character.

With the anointing of a child at baptism with the oil of chrism, we already have a sign of the presence of the Holy Spirit. Our sacramental theology clearly expounds that the grace we receive in every Sacrament is a gift of and results from the indwelling of the Holy Spirit. We are not only called to be but are the children of God because the grace we receive constitutes us in a dynamic relationship with the Father, the Son and the Holy Spirit.

The gift has to be received – creative grace is not possible without the co-operation of the person with whose spirit the Holy Spirit conspires. Our main sacramental theological problem is related precisely to the practice of infant baptism. The Fathers of the Second Vatican Council, conscious of the relationship between grace and faith and faith and grace, called for the reform of the Rites of Infant Baptism relating the sacramental grace to the faith of the parents and the Community of Faith. They also, significantly, called for the Profession of Faith, on the part of the candidates themselves in the administration of the Sacrament of Confirmation.

For the receiving of Holy Communion, confirmation is not a necessary prerequisite. It could be argued, however, that it is for the effective discharge of our missionary vocation as Christians. The gifts of the Spirit are precisely those which enable us to bear witness to the faith and fortify us for its proclamation. The congruence of the bishop, being the ordinary minister of the Sacrament, with the apostolic nature of it is plain to see.

Given that confirmation can be conferred as a Sacrament at any age, even in infancy, the pastoral question remains – when is it best administered? By 'best' I mean most fruitfully in the life of the individual and of the Church. I do not intend, now, to rehearse all the arguments for an earlier or later date or for

maintaining the practice which has been commonplace in
Scotland up to the present – namely, conferring it when children
are about to leave primary school and graduate to secondary. It
may be that circumstances differ not only as between dioceses
but within them. Who, then, will exercise the necessary pastoral
discernment? It could be the bishop who insists, for the sake of
harmony, that it be conferred at a certain age throughout the
diocese. Or it could be the parish priests, in consultation with
parents, catechists, teachers and – what is important in so
compact a diocese as this – with his neighbouring priests.

Let me be straightforward: I do not want to forestall the
present programme, in so far as it enables us to look more deeply
at the nature of this Sacrament and its ecclesial implications,
assuming that, to some extent, the changes are by way of an
experiment. In other words, we will see from practice whether
confirming children at a younger age and before Holy
Communion has a beneficial impact on their lives and on the life
of the local church. The criterion is not how many children we
can confirm but how many children's lives we can change for the
better through confirmation.

In other words, the present programme continues but on the
clear understanding that it is *ad experimentum* and that a review
will be carried out in the first instance by parish priests,
reflecting on their experience at deanery level. I want the fullest
consultation to take place. Confirmation or otherwise of the
recently introduced Archdiocesan Policy will be given only when
the fullest agreement possible has been reached, not only among
priests but also among parents and those with shared
responsibility for the preparation and presentation of candidates.

In the meantime, I will respond to any Faculty requests, both
with regard to age and timing, which are presented to me by
parish priests, though I will expect, in the case of wide
divergence from the practice which has recently been introduced,
that they have consulted parents, teachers and fellow members of
their respective deaneries, including, of course, their deans.

One of the best-kept secrets of the archdiocese is the number of Social Care Projects which it administers. The commitment over so broad a range of need and of expertise would not be possible without the engagement, at public expense, of qualified individuals and suitable premises.

The possibility which the archdiocese turned into a reality under the dynamic leadership of my predecessor, Cardinal Tom Winning, was provided by a change in government thinking, to involve the private sector as a partner in the provision of social care. We would always have to be alert to the possibility of a change in this policy, whether in theory or in practice, the latter by the withdrawal of essential funding.

It is good when the Church, which is ever ready to comment on the provision of social care or lack of it for needy groups in the community, can also show its concern practically. What we have to offer is not only a vision of what becomes the dignity of individuals but also a pool of voluntary helpers who can support the work at no extra cost to the state – and we know that cost is an inhibitor of all that would ideally be done for those in need.

I said it was one of the archdiocese's best kept secrets. I still am not fully aware of the extent of our actual engagement. This is something I hope to address in coming months. I suspect that you, likewise, are not fully conversant with what is done in your name. I would like to think that, with better knowledge, we could expand, by example and by the engagement of more of our parishioners in individual projects, the overall commitment of the Church in the Archdiocese in this field of social care.

As you know, my predecessor, in marking the 500th anniversary of the Archbishopric of Glasgow, set up a specific fund, the Pastoral Care Trust, to meet, in part, the financial needs of smaller voluntary groups within the archdiocese and elsewhere in Scotland – not only within the Catholic Church but within the community at large. This is something admirable both in its initiative and in the support it gets. This latter is largely due to your interest and co-operation and I want to take this opportunity of saying how proud I feel of the priests and people of the archdiocese who can show such generosity towards the needy both at home and abroad. As you know, there will shortly be a special collection for the Pastoral Care Trust and I can tell you, in addition, that plans are under way to seek funding elsewhere in order to enhance the fund's income. In addition, at my request this year's Cardinal Winning's Ball will devote all its profits to the Social Care Projects of the archdiocese.

This is not the occasion to go deeply into our financial situation or to enlarge on my hopes for the sound financial management of the Archdiocese – other than to say that I hope to expand the Archdiocesan Finance Committee with the addition of both clergy and lay people with an interest and experience in financial management. I will also be announcing the establishment of an Ecclesiastical Buildings Advisory Group whose task will be to look at all projects affecting our church buildings – whether they be alterations, restorations or additions – with a view to expressing an opinion on their suitability from a liturgical, architectural and artistic point of view. The report will be antecedent to other reports normally presented to the Finance Committee when permission is sought to undertake work involving expense whether parochial or archdiocesan.

There are two further areas of pastoral concern to me and to you. The first is the pastoral care of young people – those in their later teens and early twenties, prior to marriage. This is the sort of group that is represented by the St Margaret of Scotland Youth Group. I was greatly impressed with their presence and involvement with the sick at Lourdes and, likewise, with the group that represented the youth of the archdiocese at Toronto during this year's Youth World Day meeting with the Holy Father.

As one of the bishop catechists I had two catechetical sessions with two large groups of English-speaking young people, which unfortunately did not include our own from Glasgow, but which were comprised of young people of similar age and like enthusiasm. I was deeply impressed with the willingness with which they listened, asked questions and contributed to the post-catechises discussions. It suggested to me that a similar formula ought to be considered in our own Archdiocese – namely, one that brings young people together; provides them with a form of catechesis in which they can ask questions; creates liturgies in which they can fully participate; and enables them to experience a sense of solidarity and peer group support in shared social and recreational gatherings.

Since my return from Toronto I have spoken to Chris Docherty, our very able youth officer, and put to him a question, which I asked him to consider with his team, and that is whether I should offer an opportunity for young people to come together in Holy Week next year and share with me in the liturgy at the cathedral. As you know, the cathedral has a small parish congregation. In the main, it is a gathered congregation and would seem to offer a valuable opportunity to do what I am suggesting with the full support of Mgr Jim Clancy, the cathedral's administrator. I would hope that you yourselves would be ready to support such a venture.

Furthermore, I would like to see a programme of similar events being drawn up to enable young people from our secondary schools, such as might be identified by the chaplains, to enable them to come together. As young persons practising or from practising families, they could contribute to and benefit from occasional gatherings. Frankly, I would like to see us using the facilities, including the lovely chapel at Scotus for such a purpose.

The second and final pastoral observation is one that so many of you have brought to my attention and that is the need to stimulate vocations to the priesthood, both secular and religious. What we have just been speaking about – namely, our youth pastoral ministry – could and should provide the basis for our addressing this matter of vocations which is becoming increasingly urgent. It has been suggested to me that I should appoint one priest in the archdiocese, relieve him of parish duties, encourage him to form a team of helpers and give him a remit to promote vocations. Such promotion would involve his visiting schools and parishes at your invitation, meeting young people and explaining the priesthood to them. Their meeting at Scotus would expose them to the reality of a seminary and let them see that there are young men presently studying for the priesthood – people, like themselves, enthused by the desire to offer themselves to Christ in the priesthood of the Catholic Church. For the rest I rely on your own promotion of priestly vocations within your parishes and the constant reminder to the people, through prayer, of a need for more and good priests so that there will never be a lack of shepherds for the people nor people for shepherding.

This address is delivered over four sessions with short breaks in between – a chance to ask questions and take a comfort break. We finish, almost miraculously, on the dot and it is clear to me that the evening has been a success. The priests recognise their concerns and hopes – so well conveyed to me during those months of individual encounters – coming through my discourse. I myself feel released to get on with the programme I have sketched out.

With the distribution of papers inviting nominations for deans and members of the Council of Priests, the first steps are taken in setting up the necessary organs of advice and support. I have another feeling and it is one of pride swelling up within me for such a body of devoted men. I conclude the evening by hosting a dinner to mark my silver jubilee as a bishop in this great archdiocese to which I have fallen heir.

Sunday, 24 November
From Barlinnie to Bellany . . .

When an archbishop visits a jail, it can be a sub-editor's dream. 'Archbishop going to prison' makes quite a headline, as does 'Archbishop in jail'.

NOVEMBER

All sorts of jokes can be made around the wording but to be in prison is no joke. When those heavy doors open and then shut behind you, you are in a different world – not a tree in sight and why does the wind always seem to howl in places where you would expect high walls to prevent it?

Barlinnie seems very similar to the prisons I knew when I was Bishop of Aberdeen, namely Peterhead, Craiginches in Aberdeen and Porterfield in Inverness. They are all Victorian piles but I cannot help admiring the stonework of Barlinnie and the remarkably fine architecture of the earliest buildings, one of which houses the Lockerbie bomber. A small yard, little more than a cage, shows how restricted his freedom is. Without wishing to minimise in any way the atrocity that was committed more than a decade ago, I reflect that, although he may have several rooms to himself, the lack of human company must be very difficult to bear. No doubt it is the opportunity for company that helps ensure a good congregation of prisoners for mass. I suppose there must be sixty men and more, most of them young – and some very young.

The building where we assemble is a handsome purpose-built chapel with high gothic windows and an open beamed roof. The altar, placed down on floor level and not on the high stage, is adorned with a multi-coloured coverlet, the only attractive furnishing in the place.

Without wanting to appear pompous, I think, on these occasions, one should respect the congregation and I do so by bringing along a mitre and a fine vestment adorned with the logo of the archdiocese, to which I imagine most of the men belong.

A press statement issued from the office prior to my visit suggested, by the spin put on it by reporters, that I was visiting the prison in order to condemn the degrading living conditions. While I do think we have to acknowledge that these Victorian buildings have not kept pace with the living conditions even in the poorest parts of the city and that point needs to be made, I also feel that the main punishment for prisoners is their loss of freedom, not the degrading conditions.

In reality, my main purpose in visiting the prison is a pastoral one. As I explain at the beginning of the mass, prisoners are part of my flock and, prompted by Prisoners' Week which ends today, I feel I ought to be among them.

The mention of 'flock' is appropriate since the Gospel set for the day, the last Sunday in the Church's calendar, is the solemnity of Christ the King which presents Christ as the Shepherd–King. 'I will keep my flock in view' were the words that jumped out at me from the first reading from the prophet Ezekiel. But by far the most apposite passage came from the twenty-fifth chapter of St Matthew, where the Last Judgement is described in terms of a shepherd dividing the sheep from the goats, placing the former on his right hand and the latter on the left. The sheep are those who have fed the hungry, clothed the naked and visited the sick and those in prison: 'insofar as you did it to one of the least of my brethren, you did it to Me,' says the Lord (Matt. 25: 31–46).

My focus on that passage and my remarks about the need to recognise, in one another, the features of Christ seem to strike home because I am conscious that you could hear a pin drop. And, while there is some restlessness before the end of the mass, I am impressed with the general demeanour of the prisoners and the evident devotion at least of some of them and the courtesy of most.

It is, of course, an extraordinary saying that service of the needy is the service of Christ and a neglect of the needy is a neglect of Christ. The words would seem to identify the needy person with Christ himself, though recognising Christ in one another does have its implications in terms of all our behaviour.

When I was interviewed prior to the prison visit, I spoke of the need to put a greater emphasis on rehabilitation. I am, therefore, glad to see measures being undertaken to ensure humanity within Barlinnie and outside of it as well, when eventually those presently incarcerated are released. I see evidence of this. After a break for coffee, I am taken to see the games hall. There, a number of prisoners are assisting in the organisation of games for youngsters who have been invited into the prison on a visit. Parents stand huddled in a doorway watching protectively – and not without some amusement – as their offspring take part in a relay race which involves dressing up in clothes which in the main are far too big for them, with trousers around their ankles and arms lost somewhere up the sleeves. It is all part of a rehabilitation programme of which the academic aspect is evident in a neighbouring room where papers and pencils lie scattered over the tables.

There is certainly no feeling of oppression in the prison and Glasgow humour is not lacking – as we overhear a group of prisoners remarking as a priest, by the name of James Lawlor, passes them, 'There goes Jim the Tim!' (Those not conversant with Glasgow parlance should know that 'Tim' denotes an Irish Catholic.)

Coming out of the prison, I join my hands and thump the air above my head in mock exaltation at having been liberated – only to be reminded at once of the security cameras all round, no doubt picking up this somewhat 'unepiscopal' behaviour prompted by a sense of relief that the visit has gone well.

I am back at the Church of Christ the King, for 12 noon, where, earlier in the summer, I ordained Dr Frank Wilson to the priesthood with the same theme of the shepherd before me. I remind the congregation that it was from their church that I left to go to Rome to receive the pallium that is now on my shoulders. It reminds me that not only am I to be Christ-like, since that is the duty of all Christians, but that I am also to be like the good shepherd 'who has his sheep in view'. I also remind them of St Augustine's famous words, 'I am a Christian with you but a bishop for you'.

Both in the prison and in this large parish church, I draw on my Roman experience to describe the burial place of the early Christians in the subterranean catacombs. There the art of fresco painting – still in its primitive form but to be developed so marvelously all those centuries later by the renaissance and early baroque artists, including Michelangelo in the Sistine Chapel –

gave early evidence of the faith of that community. Among the most engaging images in those Roman burial-places is that of Christ the good shepherd surrounded by his sheep and bearing on his shoulders the sheep that was lost or, perhaps, the soul being borne into the rich pastures of eternal life. Certainly St Paul saw clearly and wrote eloquently both in his letter to the Romans and in his First Letter to the Corinthians of the intrinsic connection between sin and death, on the one hand, and holiness and life, on the other. 'Sin came into the world through one man and death through sin' (Rom. 5: 12). 'But in fact Christ has been raised from the dead as first fruit of those who have fallen asleep. For as by a man came death, by a man has come also the resurrection of the dead' (1 Cor. 15: 20).

The trouble with eternal life is we have no vision of it. Our imaginations are beggared. We do not have the building blocks to construct in visual manner this heavenly kingdom. Of course, lacking imagination is not to lack faith and experience itself shows us that the more we overcome sin in our lives, the greater we experience a sense of freedom and of life. In the catacombs, the dead point to the resurrection because they point to Christ, the good shepherd. This has been one of the most powerful images in Christian iconography.

After lunch in the presbytery, I make a passing call on my dentist and his wife, Nicky and Anne McCluskey, to meet, at their invitation, their lovely family. There Ronnie picks me up and we go to the Glasgow Film Theatre to see a documentary on the artist John Bellany whom we had met little over a month ago in Italy. The film is entitled *Life, Death and Resurrection* – the resurrection period being that following John's liver transplant and, in a sense, that other transplantation from Scotland to Tuscany. His powerful images, revealing so much of his own inner journey, remain haunting. And the camera lingered beguilingly on those valleys and far-off mountains of chestnut groves and trees in flower, all from a spot at which we stood so recently.

The transformation from his earlier paintings to the later is a journey out of darkness into light, a journey to which John himself bears witness. But, as we return home by car, Ronnie and I reflect on the fact that there is a chapter missing in the documentary. It is the chapter we experienced ourselves when we met up with him in Barga. If much of the darker elements of his art has been explained in terms of an inherited Calvinism, it is clear that the journey into a landscape and culture touched by Catholicism is having its effect.

I think again of the powerful image of Christ he presented to me, the intensity of the eyes and the spiritual emotion that the painting conveys, a gift of expression which, the film's commentator remarks, account for John's extraordinary artistic success. We surely now await a painting which conveys – as Raphael's marvelous 'Transfiguration of Christ' does – the glory of the resurrection. We rely on the artist all the more when our own imaginations fail us.

It has been an extraordinary day, tracking, as it has, failure and hope – a trajectory from darkness to light, in the prisoners, the parishioners and the painters who illuminate our lives, be they wordsmiths or colourists. And in their midst stands a bishop, like a shepherd among his sheep.

December

Wednesday, 25 December

Any account of an archbishop's first year in office could not possibly omit mention of one of the greatest feasts of the Church – namely, Christmas – nor should it fail to reflect on the significance of a New Year.

My predecessor had chosen to celebrate Christmas midnight mass in different parishes of the archdiocese. I decide, at least for this first year, to go to the cathedral. It had always been my practice in Aberdeen to celebrate great events in the cathedral. It is, after all, the bishop's church – the place where he has his 'cathedra' or seat.

Since the cathedral no longer serves a large parish but is, rather, a gathering place of 'refugees' (not in any technical sense!) from other parishes and visitors to the city, there was a sizeable congregation for our Christmas midnight mass last night, although the Administrator, Mgr Jim Clancy, acknowledged, over punch and mincemeat pies afterwards, that he recognised very few of the congregation. Indeed, this was marked by a preponderance of men, many of whom, judging by their appearance, may well have been seamen or refugees in the more customary sense of the word.

This morning I go first of all to St Margaret's Hospice at Clydebank where I am warmly greeted by Sr Rita, the Executive Director. As on previous occasions, she has invited the Provost of Clydebank and the many other people, medical and lay, who support the hospice in the care of the terminally ill, both professionally and through fund-raising activities. I am impressed by the number who have accepted the invitation and it must be encouraging for the patients who join them to have so many friends come to share what might be their last Christmas with them. Among the patients I meet is Joe Keenan, the father of two ardent young priests of the archdiocese. One of them, Fr Joseph, I had recently appointed to one of the poorer parishes of the city, an appointment which he embraced with enthusiasm, and the other, Fr John, is the Catholic chaplain to the University of Glasgow.

Earlier in the year, I was able to ask the Prime Minister directly whether more consideration might be given to the public support of such hospices. Not only are they needed, in themselves, if we are to care properly for those who are facing terminal illness, but they are also necessary in counteracting the drift towards euthanasia that is all too evident in mainland Europe and which is often heralded in this country by those whose understanding of individual freedom and compassion is different to our own. Indeed, this understanding is sometimes diametrically opposed to the Christian concept of duty on the part of individuals and society in the face of natural dissolution and death. I recall a very moving television programme, by the late Malcolm Muggeridge, in which he visited the home of the dying in Calcutta, founded by Mother Teresa and her Missionaries of Charity. She explained, with utter simplicity, that what the dying needed above all was love. It would not only be an intelligent but also a compassionate community that saw the need for and gave its support to hospices such as St Margaret's.

It is a similar sort of love and compassion that led to the foundation of homes for the elderly throughout the country by the Sisters of Nazareth. One of their largest is Nazereth House in Paisley Road West in Glasgow and it is there that I go following the mass at St Margaret's. The sister in charge, Sister Machar, is a friend from Aberdeen days. She is a very able superior and she has largely modernised the house. It had become my practice, since the death of my mother there in 1991, to have Christmas dinner with the Sisters of Nazereth in Aberdeen, so it seems a natural progression to do the same in Glasgow. However, first, I want to meet the seven retired priests of the diocese who live there. They are all waiting for me when I arrive and we have drinks and much pleasant chat, with the inevitable recollection of memories – mainly theirs, though I have my own contribution to make when I remind one of them that his brother had been my spiritual director for some time when I was a student in Rome. In a more formal exchange of Christmas greetings, Mgr Martin Quinlan, the Provost of the Cathedral Chapter – the most senior canon in the diocese and the one who had presented the crucifix for me to kiss at the door of the cathedral on the night of my installation – gives me a bottle of Cointreau!

Friday, 27 December

Between Christmas and New Year, I am returning somewhat surreptitiously to the Diocese of Aberdeen – not to the city itself but to Inverness where I am staying with my holiday companion of many years, Mgr Robert McDonald. We are celebrating appropriately!

Sunday, 29 December

Today I go to visit friends near Beauly. Their three children – still being young and for the first time in many years all being together during the course of my visit – have invited loads of their friends, equally young, to join them here and elsewhere during the holiday period. One of the family is having a special celebration to mark both his son's twenty-first and his wife's birthday and we have a splendid meal under canvas – a marquee, I should say, not a tent! It is beautifully decorated in the sprit of the season.

I decline an invitation to take to the floor for the 'Dashing White Sergeant' on the grounds of my advancing age. However, I become trapped between a pincer movement of invitations – if you see what I mean – and I find myself with two ladies reeling in the typical Scottish fashion. How splendid Scottish dancing is in that it can bring young and old together on the dance floor – and I really do mean together because, in the course of such a reel, you meet virtually everyone as you weave in and out in figures of eight and other steps. I learned the basics of such dances at, of all places, the Scots College Villa in Marino, in the Roman countryside, during a *villeggiatura*, or holiday break, many moons ago. On that occasion, a priest from the Isles, Canon Calum MacNeill, who was much more senior to ourselves, decided to train us for a concert piece at the Gregorian University – a real sign of the changing spirit in the staid and stately corridors in the present day successor to the Collegio Romano. It's unlikely that St Ignatius of Loyola – under whose patronage the Collegio and the Greg are placed – would have known much about Scottish country dancing but there is every reason to believe that, in his early chivalrous years, he would have learned the steps of a Navarre jig!

Tuesday, 31 December

Today, it's back to Glasgow in time for the New Year celebrations. Probably for the first time in all my years as a priest and bishop, I am alone at home when the clock strikes midnight. Soon afterwards I phone Betty Petrie, my former neighbour in Aberdeen, where I am right to assume that all the neighbours have, as they have done for many years, gathered in Betty's house to see in the New Year together.

They tell me that they miss my company and this adds to the nostalgia that I feel. I determine that never again will I take in the New Year bereft of human company. I don't normally feel lonely when alone but, on this occasion, it is different. However, at the risk of appearing over pious, I do confess to spending some time in the oratory reflecting on the year that had passed – a year full of new experiences, new challenges, new hopes – and I look forward, not without the confidence that is inspired from above, to the year ahead.

2003

January

Wednesday, 1 January

New Year's morning and back again to the company of religious sisters, old folk and retired priests as I go off to celebrate mass at the Convent of the Little Sisters of the Poor at Robroyston. They have a lovely chapel there and a beautiful, purpose-built house. I have a splendid meal, no different – probably not even in the number of Brussels sprouts – from what is being enjoyed all around me.

We are served by the sisters and their supporting staff – the sisters not eating their meals until all the residents have been served. In this way, they remind themselves of the extra vow they make which is to serve the poor. I think the residents of St Joseph's Home at Robroyston are poor in only one sense – that they have spent most of the sum of the earthly days given to them. What a privilege to be in a house where the future is not something to be shunned but welcomed.

I leave St Joseph's, as I left Nazareth House a week ago, laden both with good wishes expressed both verbally and in liquid form – not to mention chocolates and other venial temptations to gluttony!

Sunday, 12 January

Intent as I am on what I am saying and alert as I am to the large congregation spread all around me, I am nonetheless conscious all the time that I stand in the pulpit of St Mungo's Cathedral this afternoon – the vigil of St Mungo's feast. It is a significant occasion.

It might be too much to say that this is a historic occasion – though it must be the first time since the Reformation that a Catholic Archbishop of Glasgow has joined the Minister of Glasgow Cathedral and leaders of the other churches, who have their origins in the Reformation settlements, to honour St Mungo. This is the

1400th anniversary of his death and burial. Dr William Morris KCBO, the Minister – and Minister for many years – of St Mungo's has readily agreed to our holding an ecumenical service on the vigil of the feast under the auspices of Glasgow Churches Together. We met just prior to Christmas in the chapter room of the cathedral and there mapped out the service, based upon Vespers or Evening Prayers, and incorporating music with which the St Mungo's Singers are familiar. This choir, under the direction of Mgr Gerry Fitzpatrick, fulfils the function of an archdiocesan choir and performs on big occasions. In the event, they fill the high vaulting of the cathedral with glorious sound.

The weather today is cold and wet but this does not deter a congregation of some 600 people from gathering, many of whom have responded to an invitation which I incorporated into my first pastoral letter since becoming Archbishop of Glasgow and which was published this weekend.

Several strands come together in the weaving of that letter. What I called an 'insightful' editorial in *The Herald* on 4 January helped me to address the issue of sectarianism. A remark by the First Minister, Jack McConnell, relating to shared campuses for schools proved to be the trigger for what appeared to be a concerted attack by others on Catholic education on the grounds that it was either a contributory factor to, or a means of continuing, sectarian divisions within the community. Drawing from a table of comparative exam results of schools in the more deprived areas of Scotland, I have been able to show that, as I put it, 'Catholic schools are punching above their weight' in addressing the cultural and spiritual poverty that are either a concomitant factor in or a result of the endemic physical poverty of large tracts of this city.

It is a historical fact that, in the years following the First World War, strong divisions and antipathies grew up between the Catholic and Protestant Irish or Scots communities in Glasgow, leading to the notorious report by the Church and Nation Committee of the Church of Scotland called 'The Menace of the Irish Race to our Scottish Nationality'. This document advocated deporting Irish people receiving poor relief and supported job discrimination in public works in favour of native Scots since, according to the report's authors, 'Scotland was over-gorged with Irishmen'. In this most recent onslaught it seemed once again as if, somehow or other, the Catholic community should take responsibility for divisions in society, with the solution lying in the dismantling of the Catholic school system. In the pastoral letter, I promised that 'Gospel values underpin and inform the education provided in our Catholic schools. I intend to defend them from all such unjust attacks that caricature them as nurseries or breeding grounds of bigotry.' I conclude, however, that it isn't sufficient simply to counter the attack on the schools. We have to offer a vision of the Churches working together to tackle the true roots of cultural and spiritual deprivation through a rededication of ourselves to what is, after all, the mission of the Church – namely, 'the preaching of His word and the praising of His name'. These are the means whereby, in the words of the city's motto, 'Glasgow will flourish'.

My reflections in St Mungo's Cathedral, on this outwardly cold but internally warm Sunday afternoon, are based upon the theme of my pastoral letter and, in some parts, I quote it verbatim. Given the setting, I stress the more ecumenical aspect of the commitment.

In a city that is often harshly judged for its manifestations of intolerance, I feel a very special responsibility rests on the believers in Christ to work together, visibly together, for the benefit of all Glaswegians.

The St Mungo anniversary to which I have already alluded gives us the opportunity to do so. Today, our 'praising of His name' of the city motto should resonate with other Churches and find an echo in other faiths represented in the city.

My meetings with my fellow Church leaders have convinced me that we have a marvelous opportunity to mark this St Mungo 1400th anniversary year together, with special events at all levels of parish and city life, and we look to the Lord Provost and city fathers for the promotion of the latter.

This first event is a clear signal of the desire of Glasgow's Christians to put aside any lingering animosities and journey together. To use the words made famous by Pope John Paul in this very city twenty-one years ago: 'Can we not make that journey together, hand in hand?'

Together we can achieve much. Separated we are seriously weakened.

The other Church leaders and I are photographed beforehand at the tomb of St Mungo, in the crypt of the cathedral, and now we walk together, in procession, slowly through the choir, to greet people as they issue from under the ancient rood screen, at the side of which the Christmas crib is still prominently displayed. Dr Morris turns to tell me that he has long looked forward to a day such as this and it is evident that many others echo his sentiments as they shake hands with us on their way out. I feel we can only go forward and already there are plans afoot for walking 'hand in hand', as Pope John Paul put it, throughout the Year of St Mungo.

During the course of these celebrations, an opportunistic BBC reporter and cameraman interview and film me for a brief item which is to appear later on news bulletins. What has been picked up is an article of mine in today's *Sunday Herald* in which I trace the possibility of reproductive cloning – the latest 'aberration' in the field of human bio-technology – back to the original decision of the UK government to allow in vitro fertilisation. I thought that this would have been an evident enough point, hardly needing anything more than my mention of it and of subsequent logical steps in order to remind people of where we had come from and where we were likely to be going. But it seems as if, somehow or other, the point has been missed or no longer remembered.

The article had started as a letter recognising as valid the concerns of Dr Ian Gibson, Chairman of the Commons Science and Technology Committee, over the prospect of a trade developing in human embryos. But, in the event, the paper was glad to have a full article, allowing a better development of the theme.

I'm forever reminded, on these occasions, of the saying of one of my colleagues, Fr George Donaldson, a moral theologian and lecturer at Scotus College: 'Mario, we may be wrong but, if we are, we're consistently wrong!' I don't think anyone could disagree with the internal logic of our case. However, I do recognise that there is an element in our argument that is not shared by everyone but which is utterly fundamental to us – our conviction of the unique character of each individual human being and the unconditional respect for the life of each from conception to natural death. This is based upon our belief in God, the instruction given in the Judaeo–Christian moral inheritance and the love shown for each of us in the life and death of Our Lord Jesus Christ. On such a basis, the creation of human beings in the laboratory and the saving of some at the expense of many others deeply offend against this ethical principle, even where the results of such procedures are welcomed into the human family and loved. And we would be acting contrary to that very ethic should we refuse such a welcome.

To underline that point, I recall, at the beginning of my article, the following.

When Louise Brown, the world's first test-tube baby was born, one of the first assurances of prayers for the new-born child came from the relatively unknown Patriarch of Venice, Albino Luciani, who, within months, was elected Pope as John Paul I – a pontificate lasting thirty-three days. His words raised eyebrows. Was it appropriate for such a message to come from a senior Catholic churchman, given the Church's firm opposition to the very processes that had led to the baby's birth? On reflection, it is clear that Patriarch Luciani was perfectly right to offer his prayers for the baby's well-being. Irrespective of the processes, the baby was, and is, a human being.

This episode came to mind when it was recently announced – that 'Baby Eve' had been born – reputedly the world's first cloned baby. To a cloned baby, as to any newborn infant, is due the fullness of respect and care that is the right of every human being. But, in recent days, the veracity of this claim has been questioned and I join innumerable scientists, ethicists and politicians round the world in hoping that it is no more than a publicity stunt by an obscure sect. The attempted cloning of a human being is fraught with danger both in its processes and in its results with regard to the physical and psychological well-being of the cloned person.

We would not be addressing this difficult question, however, were it not for the fact that we have already crossed several moral boundaries before finally coming to an instinctive halt at the brink of reproductive cloning. One moral problem has succeeded another. The first step on this nightmarish journey was the British Government's acceptance of in vitro fertilisation – namely, the production of human beings in a petri dish. It is often forgotten that, for every child brought to birth using these techniques, several embryos will have died, been frozen or beendestroyed in the process. An even more ominous step was taken when the same government allowed for destructive experimentation on human embryos. The next step was the removal of stem cells from what have been appallingly referred to as 'superfluous embryos', destroying them in the process. Such procedures, in turn, paved the way for so-called 'therapeutic cloning' – the creation of human embryos for a maximum period of fourteen days, during which time their stem cells are removed, killing them. Then, just last week, the *Sunday Herald* revealed the prospect of a trade in human embryos and how

> The Medical Research Council which is setting up the UK Stem Cell Bank to store cells for spare body parts, has written to selected IVF clinics offering them money to pay for a nurse co-ordinator who would encourage patients to donate their embryos for stem-cell research.

This opening-up of a market in human life strikes me as simply a logical progression ever further into this bio-ethical house of horrors.

JANUARY

Dr Ian Gibson may well be concerned. I admire his courage in standing up to the Medical Research Council and questioning their proposal. However, I would hope that his concern would extend beyond a trade in human embryos to the very notion of providing human embryos for medical research in the first place.

All the steps outlined above have been taken on the grounds of a purely utilitarian ethic. When followers of such an ethic find that a particular course of action is useful, they describe it as good. The motivation is generally sentiment. By that, I mean not causing pain to anyone and bringing happiness to others.

Of course, sentiment is purely subjective and the judgement about bringing happiness to others is notoriously relative. Such arguments undoubtedly serve commercial purposes but do not provide a foundation for sound legislation that has the benefit of the wider community in view. I will be told – and have been told by medical researchers who know better – that an embryo at this stage is only a blob of cells. I will be told that I would be inhibiting research that was necessary for the curing of a number of genetic diseases. There are other sources of stem cells, however – for example, in the placenta and umbilical cord and, indeed, within adult bone marrow. Only last week, scientists, at the University of Rostock in Germany, reported using stem cell injections to aid the recovery of heart attack victims. The stem cells were obtained from the patients' own bone marrow.

Of course, nobody likes to be told that they are doing is wrong, particularly when they are so well motivated. But doing wrong they are. In all these cases scientists are subjecting human beings, however young, to destructive procedures: making one embryo, a human being in an as yet undeveloped state, the means to another human being's end; the potential of one subjected to the potential of another.

The argument from sentiment – if that is to be the basis of one's moral philosophy – is unassailable. The fourteen-day-old embryo feels no pain, while the developed embryo, before and after birth, can and does. But it was sentiment – or rather the lack of it – which enabled the Nazi regime to decide on and carry through the horrific policy of liquidation of the Jewish people. And many other horrors throughout history, even recent history, have been based on purely utilitarian arguments, or on a philosophy that has, for a whole range of motives, subjugated one group of human beings to the benefit of another.

The only sound principle we have known for equitable law and the defence of human life is that no individual human being is expendable. Or, to put it in a more traditional form, no innocent may be killed. And this is still – surprisingly, despite all these aberrations – the basis of our law. When that principle, even in its most extenuated form, is ignored, we do not progress but, rather, regress as a civilised people. I take no pleasure in noting that those who can help us most can sometimes harm us not the least.

By happy chance, I was a guest, along with Archbishop Keith O'Brien, at the first annual dinner of the Catholic Medical Association at the Corinthian, in the heart of Glasgow's Merchant City last Friday, and there I was able to alert the doctors and guests present to the publication of the article. I also asked for their support in line with one of the stated purposes of their association – namely, to inform themselves of the Church's teaching on medico-moral matters and offer their support in the formulation and presentation of it.

Monday, 13 January

I celebrate mass this evening in our own cathedral of St Andrew, along with members of the Cathedral Chapter, the new deans and many other priests and people to mark St Mungo's feast day. I note the coincidence of other significant anniversaries.

It would be remiss of me not to note that this year is also the 400th anniversary of the death of the last Catholic Archbishop of Glasgow at the time of the Reformation. James Beaton, recognising the collapse of the moral authority of the medieval Church and knowing that the power of the Crown vested in the young Queen Mary Stuart, Queen Dowager of France, would not be sufficient to prevent the Church being despoiled by the many who coveted its lands and its influence, took with him to Paris the archives and treasures of his cathedral. There he exercised a role as ambassador both for Mary Stuart and James VI. When he died in 1603, he left his property and salvaged treasures to the Scots College of which he became, thereby, the second founder. We will be celebrating its fourth centenary later this year in Paris.

I also note that it was just over a hundred years (101, to be exact) since the death of the first Roman Catholic archbishop in the restored hierarchy, Archbishop Charles Eyre.

With the Restoration of the Scottish Catholic hierarchy in 1878, there was in Glasgow once again a Catholic archbishop in the person of Charles Eyre, who died just over a hundred years ago. It would be legitimate to think of him as the second Founder of the See since he did so much to ensure that the Catholic faith was preached and nourished in the minds and hearts of that increasing body of poor men and women who came to Glasgow at the time of the Industrial Revolution from the Highlands of Scotland and the green shores of Ireland – 'a great haul of fish'!

Many before and after Archbishop Eyre have paid out their nets as fishers of men here on the banks of the Clyde. It is almost exactly a year since I was sent to join them, in a line of succession that goes back directly to Archbishop Eyre and indirectly to St Mungo himself. I am deeply conscious both of the privilege and of the responsibility of my office.

It seems the appropriate setting for a profession of faith and an oath of loyalty to the Church in the person of the Holy Father and the College of Bishops, such as is normally taken by those who assume important offices within the Church. I share the first part with the nine new deans, a few of whom are represented by proxies since they themselves are on holiday – a not unfamiliar choice of holiday time for the clergy after the busy lead-up to Christmas and the New Year. The appointment and commissioning of these deans, whom I describe as 'leaders among their fellows', mark the first step in the structural reorganisation of the archdiocese, one which had, indeed, been, to some extent, anticipated by my predecessor.

As I stand by the draughty cathedral doors at the end of mass, I am feeling resplendent in a multi-coloured vestment with matching mitre created by Netta Ewing and worked on by members of the St Albert Embroidery Guild, some of whose faithful members also form part of the St Mungo Singers. A little Glasgow woman, whom I had teased about her red hat outside these very doors on the day my appointment was made public, waves it in front of me cheekily as she leaves. The warm humour of what I can now call 'my Glasgow folk' is unfailing.

Tuesday, 14 January

Today is the funeral of Joe Keenan. He was one of the patients I spoke to on Christmas day at St Margaret's Hospice. The funeral is one of the most moving events I have experienced in a long while, such is the respect in which he was held by the parish and such is the love that he engendered in his family.

Wednesday, 15 January

As I write this I am acutely aware that it is a year to the day – and to the hour – since my appointment was made public. I am travelling, along with Gerry Beechey who acts as my chauffeur, to the Southern General Hospital in Glasgow. It is an odd way to celebrate the anniversary. When I remark on this to Gerry, we look at the clock and my mind immediately goes back to those first moments in what seems to me a year and more ago, though to others, to whom I have mentioned it, it appears to have been a much shorter period of time.

JANUARY

I suppose it's the novelty of so many of the experiences and, indeed, the very number of them that makes the year seem longer. And, if I were in any doubt as to what the year has achieved, I only need to look at *The Scotsman* today with its headline, 'Archbishop Conti Speaks on Doubts, Death and Fragility of Belief'.

Before leaving the house, Ronnie phones to warn me of this headline and to prepare me not only for an article in the S2 section of the paper, resulting from an interview with Katie Grant, but also a very sympathetic editorial in the main section of the newspaper. But what am I doing marking the anniversary in so inappropriate a manner? The truth is that I am not going to visit a sick priest, comfort a friend or make an official visit to the hospital. I'm going in for an operation – albeit not an emergency but, nonetheless, one that was advised – and it just happens that this is the first available date which suits both me and the surgeon.

The reference to 'death' in the headline was neither prompted by this anticipated hospitalisation nor, in the circumstances, a trigger to fear. Those who know hospitals as I do, both as a visitor and a patient, will readily understand how supportive and comforting doctors and nurses are and how tenderly they act towards their patients. While it is something we now almost take for granted, it deserves to be acknowledged gratefully at every opportunity. One by one, they come in to see me, disturbing my reading of the paper which by now has been purchased for me.

'What would you like to be called?' I suggest 'Bishop' might be easiest on the tongue. Certainly no need for 'Archbishop' or 'Your Grace' and certainly not 'Archie'. Somehow or other, I don't think that one quite suits me! In the event, I get every imaginable form address!

The questioners and the questions come fast, one upon another. It is comforting that there are so many questions to which I can answer 'no', though I notice there are none referring to my mental capacity or my psychological balance. Perhaps the question, 'Do you know what operation you are going to have?', is intended as a catch-all, on the answer to which a whole series of observations might be made. I certainly notice that there is a whole page of faint blue lines on which a response might be relegated.

Then enthusiastic operators, of inscrutable mein, bring in machines to test blood pressure and check the heart. And then there are the senior nurses and junior doctors who pronounce me fit for the operation, remarking, to my satisfaction, that, despite all the bits that I have already lost, I appear sound! Glasgow has not been sold 'a pig in a poke', as one of my erstwhile priests might have said. On the contrary, *The Scotsman* opined – albeit by reference to a different set of standards – a man for the hour: 'Come the times, come the man.'

When I read a description of the times, I could feel daunted by the judgement:

> Today the Church of Rome finds itself beset by new and unexpected problems: priestly scandals, dramatic shifts in western social mores, a falling away of vocations. And the suffering brought about by AIDS in the third world . . .

The editorial notes that the interview which it carries reveals a 'very different [man] from the late and much-loved Cardinal Winning'. In that both the interview and *The Scotsman*'s editorial confirm the predictions made exactly a year before. the editorial shows perspicacity in stating: 'Following Cardinal Winning's success in reintegrating the Catholic Church into the mainstream of Scottish life and giving it influence, some might have been tempted to rest at that and turn to matters pastoral.' I confess to that being a strong temptation! But the editorial's conclusion is comforting: 'Archbishop Conti rightly senses that the tide of change is rushing at too great a torrent for a central leader of Scotland's Catholics not to take the risk of addressing difficult issues. He should be respected for doing so.'

In the light of all the controversies, relating to bio-ethics and sectarianism, over the weekend and, indeed, over the last month, I find unexpected satisfaction in reading this. What then about

'Doubts, Death and the Fragility of Belief' of the front-page headline? This referred to a passage in the interview:

Occasionally [he] wakes up wondering whether his belief in God stems from real conviction or from so many people being dependent on him. 'I have doubts,' he says, 'particularly relating to the afterlife. You see I have an imagination and an imagination is no help whatsoever when contemplating the afterlife – indeed, it is a source of difficulty. One has sometimes to fall back on naked faith.'

It is true. Being a bishop does not cushion a man from the experience of ordinary Christians – in which respect, a bishop is also ordinary. Nor does it give him any special revelation to make the act of faith more comfortable. On the contrary, the very knowledge that so many depend upon his faith, the reference to it as a sort of fixed pole within the Church and the assumption that he knows the answers to the challenges of faith make the holding of faith even more difficult.

On the other hand, a bishop is surrounded by people of faith which is sometimes expressed with vehemence and, at other times, gently held with remarkable perseverance. I recall my mother's own 'uncluttered faith' – the words I used in my homily at her funeral. *The Scotsman* contrast my faith with my 'mother's "utter confidence" that on death she would meet her friends and hear heavenly music'. One of those lovely little providences that so often come to us at the time of death – I mean, the death of those we love – came when I was with her a couple of weeks before she died and she heard 'beautiful music'. I was hushed from speaking in order that she might hear it better. Since her hearing was less good than mine and I heard not a thing, I could only conclude that it had reached her on different wavelengths – those which already emanated from the furthest shore.

Since death has a final ring about it, perhaps it would be appropriate to end this account of my first year as Archbishop of

Glasgow with these thoughts. The last chapter in life's book, death, is not the end of everything and certainly, in the Christian vision, it is only the death of what we presently experience. But there is another reason for ending on this note since it is also the one I struck at the very beginning of my time as Archbishop of Glasgow. When asked what I thought was the most important issue facing Christians today, I answered, unhesitatingly, that it was 'the question of faith'. In the interview published today, I state that, when all else fails – most of all the imagination on which we depend so much – 'one has sometimes to fall back on naked faith'. For it is within the parameters of what we have experienced and continue to experience that we feel comfortable and not in another mode of life which our unknowing minds can dress up with all sorts of fantastic images.

St John the Apostle remarked, appositely, 'What we are to be in the future has not yet been revealed. All we know is that when it is we will be like Him' (1 John 3: 2). Given what I said at the beginning and again in interview, I am pleased to read in the editorial the following passage:

> Some may be surprised at the Archbishop's ready admission of having the normal doubts that afflict any believer. But then, as he explains, doubt and faith are not mutually exclusive. For him faith is what ultimately conquers natural doubt. In modern times the norm has been otherwise. Many Church ministers square the circle by lurching from doubt into professing a strange secular Christianity, keeping the ethics but jettisoning heaven.

I continue the quotation with some measure of embarrassment.

> Again, the archbishop takes an intellectually brave stand. By acknowledging human doubt, while being intent on still keeping God, he may be opening up a much-needed debate in this spiritually parched land.

JANUARY

At the moment of writing I know neither the outcome of tomorrow's operation, nor the future of faith in our society and my ability to address the issues which flow from it. However, what I am confident of is that I won't be alone any more than I have been alone during the course of this first year, deprived neither of companionship nor of help from above.

My prayer of 'Oh Help!' has not lacked a generous answer.

INDEX